Dancing with Impermanence

Buddhist Wisdom for Life and Loss

Margaret Meloni, PhD

Copyright ©2025 Margaret Meloni

All rights reserved. No part of this publication may be reproduced, distributed, or transmitted in any form or by any means, including photocopying, recording, or other electronic or mechanical methods, without the prior written permission of the publisher, except in the case of brief quotations embodied in reviews and certain other non-commercial uses permitted by copyright law.

www.margaretmeloni.com

ISBN paperback: 978-1-7329075-8-4
ISBN ebook: 978-1-7329075-9-

Dedication

If you're here because you're seeking support on your grief journey, then this is for you.

If you're here because you are looking for support as you move closer to death, then this is for you.

If you're here out of curiosity about death, or grief, or Buddhism, then this is for you.

If you're here, then I thank you, and I appreciate you, and this is for you.

To all beings, may you be well, may you be happy, may you be at ease, and free from suffering.

Table of Contents

Dedication iii

Abbreviations vii

Introduction ix

Chapter 1: Facing Death with Grace and Mindfulness 1
Can You Wish Mettā to the Dying 3
If You Want to Be Ready for Death, Train Like an Athlete 9
Maraṇasati is For All Of Us 15
Nine Simple Ways to Contemplate Death 20
Soothing the Fear of Death: Lessons from Nakula's Mother 24
Our Pets, Our Teachers 28
The Art of Caring: Embracing the Journey of Providing Love Without Expectations 32
Nobody Gets Out of This Alive 36

Chapter 2: Rebirth, Karma, and Letting Go 40
Please Don't Come Back 42
The Problem with Ghosts 46
Responsibility and Rebirth 50
Rebirth and Right View: A Personal Journey 54
Matters of Mettā and Merit 57

Chapter 3: Grief as a Path to Understanding 63
Grief and the Four Noble Truths 64
Are More People the Answer? 68
On Receiving the Gifts of Impermanence, Clinging, and Aversion ... 72
Let Clinging Be Your Teacher 76

Chapter 4: The Wisdom of Impermanence 82
Death and Equanimity 83

The Promise of Impermanence..87
Impermanence is In Sight..91
It's the Little Things 94
Dancing Around Death: Meeting Denial with Courage and
Compassion..97
We Are the Flowers in the Garden...101

Chapter 5: Cultivating Compassion and Resilience 105
To Say Goodbye to Suffering, Say Hello to Difficult Emotions 106
Where There Is Grief, Let There Be Compassion 110
When It Comes to Grief, It's Come as You Are 114
Be Your Ally in Times of Loss...118
On Homecomings and Release from Suffering – None of This is Easy
....123
Who MOST Deserves YOUR Compassion 126

Chapter 6: Everyday Dharma: Lessons from Life 131
Keep Your Eyes on Your Own Paper.......................................133
What You Have is Now...137
Remembering the Whole Person: Honor and Celebrate the Life of a
Loved One..141
The Perfect Way to Commemorate a Death Day..................146
Whose Karma is This? 149
Of Rainbows and Sea Turtles: Letting Memories Guide and Heal Us
....153
Something is Missing, Because Someone is Missing...........156

Conclusion 160

Abbreviations

These are the abbreviations used for the Pāli Buddhist Texts, which may be quoted throughout this book.

AN	Aṅguttara Nikāya
Dhp	Dhammapada
DN	Dīgha Nikāya
Jat	Jātaka
MN	Majjhima Nikāya
SN	Saṃyutta Nikāya
Sn	Sutta Nipāta
Thag	Theragāthā
Ud	Udāna
Iti	Itivuttaka

Introduction

This book represents five years of my grief journey. And five years of sharing my path with readers of the *Death Dhamma* column on Buddhistdoor Global (https://www.buddhistdoor.net/)

Writing about death and grief, and Buddhism, has been as much for myself as it has been for others. Perhaps more so. There were many months when I wondered, "What is there to say?" How can there be anything new about death? Inevitably, some idea or topic came to light. I am not proclaiming any of these ideas to be new. Each column was motivated by a discussion, an experience, an observation, or a teaching. Even though each of our experiences is unique to us, we share challenges around understanding impermanence, clinging, and aversion. We are each trying to find a way to continue life without the support of some of our loved ones, and while developing an understanding that we, too, must die.

I offer these readings to you as a way to support you on your journey. In selecting these specific articles for you, I hope to show you that:

- You are not alone

- The Buddha's teachings will offer comfort and support

- Life and death are full of unusual experiences

- Grief is a journey, not a destination

- Your practice will sustain you

- Compassion is critical

- You are resilient

How do you approach this book and these articles? The easiest answer is any way that makes sense to you. You might close your eyes and put a finger on the contents and see what happens.

You might browse the topic categories or the article titles and read what pulls you in. Or take on a category or section at a time.

Assigning sections or categories to this article was not an exact science. Some fit neatly within a specific area, and others could have gone in multiple areas. At some point, I decided and kept moving. What follows is a brief description of each, and the type of support waiting for you in that specific section.

Facing Death with Grace and Mindfulness – This first section is meant to acknowledge that you might have a healthy fear of death. Perhaps you know that your death or the death of a loved one is imminent. Maybe, you are acting as a caretaker for someone who is ill. Facing Death with Grace and Mindfulness is here to help you look at death and the thoughts and emotions you are experiencing.

Rebirth, Karma, and Letting Go – Whether or not you believe in rebirth, this section will help you to consider what happens after we die. It will provide some perspective on how some Buddhists view rebirth, because we do not all agree. It will also give you some ideas on how to send good wishes to your dead loved ones and encourages you to think about ghosts.

Grief as a Path to Understanding – You might find this section to be short and bittersweet. Experiencing grief is a mixed bag. You can try to ignore your grief, or repress it, but one way or another it will surface. The articles in this section serve as a reminder that your Buddhist practice is here to help you, and that your experiences with grief are part of your path.

The Wisdom of Impermanence – One of our most challenging lessons as humans is to acknowledge that things will change. There is a proverb, "Man plans and God laughs." Feel free to reinterpret that as "Humans plan and karma laughs." Not because you should not have plans. Plan with awareness, knowing that things will change. Use the small things, like the life cycle of a flower, to prepare you for something like street closures on your commute. In turn, shifting traffic patterns help you practice handling other surprises. Each time something is different from what you expected, you receive an opportunity to practice for sickness, aging, and death.

Cultivating Compassion and Resilience – Visit this section when you need to remind yourself that none of this is easy. You are a human being; you love your pets and your people and certain aspects of your life. When someone you love experiences difficulty, you probably extend that person some compassion. Be someone you love and send yourself some compassion.

Everyday Dharma: Lessons from Life – Together, we share some common experiences. We have loved, we have lost our loves, and we have moved forward on our respective journeys. Not all of our experiences will be the same. This section captures some of the lessons I have learned. Some of these were unexpected, and some were just part of a "normal" life. Remember, that normal is different for each of us.

Thank you for sharing this path with me.

In gratitude and with much *metta*,

Margaret Meloni

Chapter 1

Facing Death with Grace and Mindfulness

─────●─────

This section invites you to approach death as a natural part of life. An event that we all share, greeting it with open awareness, inner balance, and a tender heart. Here you'll find down-to-earth guidance and thoughtful reflections on how to prepare for your final chapter—and how to help others with theirs.

In this collection of writings, themes of fear of death and dying are met with kindness and deep reflection. You'll encounter practical suggestions, philosophical musings, and personal stories that illuminate the path of facing mortality with presence, compassion, and grace.

At its core, death is a universal teacher, reminding you to live each moment fully and fearlessly.

- Loving-kindness practices (*metta*) nurture the heart, opening you to boundless compassion.

- Mindfulness of death (*maraṇasati*) trains your mind to remain steady and clear.

- Embracing death as part of life's natural flow can soothe anxiety and uncover profound peace.

Use this chapter as a gentle exploration of your thoughts and fears about death.

CAN YOU
WISH METTĀ TO THE DYING

Your friend is dying. Is *mettā* appropriate?

Perhaps you sign your correspondence by saying, "With *mettā*."

Or as you leave your meditation group, you say, "May you be well, may you be happy, may you be at ease, and free from suffering."

One day, you realize, "I just wished that my terminally ill friend would be well. Was that the right thing for me to say?" Or you wonder, "Am I a hypocrite when I wish my dying friend freedom from suffering, knowing that death can come with emotional and physical suffering? Am I in denial?"

True *mettā* is the ability to want others to experience safety, happiness, comfort, and good health, without expecting anything in return. Often, without them even knowing that you are sending these wishes. Yet your friend is dying. Is your *mettā* inappropriate? Or a waste of time?

In *The Sublime Attitudes / A Chanting Guide*, *mettā* is expressed in this way:

Sabbe sattā sukhitā hontu.
May all living beings be happy.

Sabbe sattā averā hontu.
May all living beings be free from animosity.

Sabbe sattā abyāpajjhā hontu.
May all living beings be free from oppression.

Sabbe sattā anīghā hontu.
May all living beings be free from trouble.

Sabbe sattā sukhī attānaṁ pariharantu.
May all living beings look after themselves with ease.

The chant ends with:

Sotthī hontu nirantaraṁ.
May you forever be well.

Nobody will forever be well unless you reconsider what it means to be well.

You need to let go of the idea that being well and free from suffering means never experiencing pain, illness, or death. That is unrealistic. The *Mahāparinibbāna Sutta* shows us that even the Buddha was subject to pain and impermanence:

Having eaten Cunda's meal (this I've heard),
He suffered from a grave illness, painful, deathly.
From eating a meal of 'pig's delight'
Grave sickness assailed the Teacher,

Having purged, the Lord then said:
'Now I'll go to Kusinārā town.' (DN 16.4.20)

After the death of the Buddha, the Brahmā Sahampati says:

All beings in the world, all bodies, must break up:
Even the Teacher, peerless in the human world,
The mighty Lord and perfect Buddha has passed away. (DN 16.6.10)

Sākka, the ruler of the devas, says:

Impermanent are compounded things, prone to rise and fall,
Having risen, they're destroyed, their passing truest bliss. (DN 16.6.10)

What does it mean to send well-wishes to your dying friend? It means to wish freedom from suffering. Of course, you do not want him or her to have extensive physical pain or mental anguish. On a deeper level, you wish that your friend experiences liberation. That is the real goal of the teachings. That is what it means to be free from suffering.

And how is liberation its core? Here, the teachings have been taught by me to my disciples for the utterly complete destruction of suffering. Through liberation, one experiences those teachings in just the way that I have taught them to my disciples for the utterly complete destruction of suffering. It is in this way that liberation is its core. (AN IV 245:3)

Suffering comes from clinging or attachment. The cessation of suffering is achieved through the termination of attachment. The way to release yourself from attachment is by following the Noble Eightfold Path. You are encouraging your friend on the path. Your wish is that he or she can become free from craving.

Yes, send *mettā*.

In *Mettā Bhavana: Loving-Kindness Meditation*, Venerable Dhammarakkhita teaches a type of flexibility in sending *mettā*. He shares a story of how, once using the internet, he realized that millions of other people were probably using the internet at the same time. And this prompted him to wish, "May everyone using the internet now be happy and peaceful."

If you need to change your phrasing to feel comfortable, then do it. What is important is your intention. To accept illness and death, not to hope against it. What does it mean for you to wish goodwill to someone who is dying? It means to be able to wish him or her a peaceful death and the ability to face death skillfully, with non-attachment and right view. Your *mettā* is the wish that he or she will experience true liberation. You are most likely to be the biggest beneficiary of your caring wishes.

When the Buddha directs his monks:

And toward the world
one should develop loving-kindness,
a state of mind without boundaries—
above, below, and across—
unconfirmed, without enmity, without adversaries. (Sn 8.150)

This direction is for their benefit. It helps the monks overcome a fear of the spirits that are harassing them in the forest. And once the monks generate thoughts of goodwill toward the spirits, their relationship becomes a friendship.

To extend *mettā* to others is to open your heart to others and to overcome your selfishness. Your ability to wish goodwill to others brings you closer to conquering ill will. Maintaining a mind free of hatred is so essential that in the "Simile of the Saw," the Buddha encourages his monks to develop a mind that resists hate, even toward those who would cut them apart with a two-handled saw.

When you can sincerely wish that all others be well, you have shown that you can conquer hatred. When you consistently wish *mettā* to all, you leave behind resentment and animosity. Now, you have a mind that is open and ready to advance toward the end of suffering.

For in this world hatred is never
Allayed by further acts of hate.
It is allayed by non-hatred;
That is the fixed and ageless law. (MN 126.6)

This is an opportunity for you to direct your goodwill to your reactions toward death.

Open your heart to death and overcome the fear of losing your friend, of losing others, and of your eventual demise. *Mettā* practice might lead you to overcome your aversion to death, resulting in your cessation of attachment.

The foundation of a healthy *mettā* practice begins with yourself. And your friend is dying. And with his or her death comes grief, and grief is suffering. May YOU be well, may YOU be free from suffering.

References

Ṭhānissaro Bhikkhu. 1994. *A Chanting Guide*. Valley Center, CA: The Dhammayut Order in the USA.

Ven. Dhammarakkhita. 2001. *Metta Bhavana: Loving-Kindness Meditation*. Nakhon Pathom, Thailand: Dhammodaya Meditation Centre.

IF YOU WANT TO BE READY FOR DEATH, TRAIN LIKE AN ATHLETE

Professional athletes train for significant events. Weightlifters rely on strengthening their core; yoga practitioners also build a stable and flexible core. One day, you will deal with death. Why not be prepared? Failing to think about death is like running a marathon without training. You might make it, but it is going to be exceptionally painful. Like the marathon, death will probably still be difficult, but with some specific training, you can rely on your core to help you face your death or navigate the loss of a loved one.

You may think, "I'll deal with that when the time comes." That is your right. However, again, this is like choosing to run that marathon with no training. Even though you rarely even jog around the block, you go out there and attempt to run all 26 miles and 385 yards. You might make it to the finish line. But it is going to hurt.

Death is difficult, and some of us come from a culture in which we turn our heads away from death. We grit our teeth and get through it. As you move through life, you will have more and more experiences with death. You can choose to accept this as part of your life, or you can spend more time in denial. Do not waste your energy.

Make the day not in vain,
a little or a lot.
However much

the day passes,
that's how much less
is life.
Your last day approaches.
This isn't your time
to be heedless. (Thag 6.13)

The clock is ticking. The date for that marathon approaches. An athlete follows a training program designed to build his or her strength and endurance. Each part of that program is geared toward setting him or her up to participate in a specific event successfully.

Suppose you faced the death of a close family member at an early age. Consider revisiting your training and becoming a coach to others.

If you were introduced to death more conventionally, perhaps, as a child, you dealt with the loss of your favorite pet. Then, later, a grandparent. Or one of your friends had a death in the family. You have begun your training, and now it is time for you to get back to work.

Training Level One: Impermanence

If you follow the lesson on impermanence to its natural conclusion, it is not just your thoughts and emotions that are rising and falling. Everything is rising and falling. Every one of us rises and ultimately falls. It is important to remember that *everyone* is going to experience death.

Recognize that everything will change. We are *all* subject to old age, sickness, and death. Old age is a gift. The more you can become comfortable with the knowledge that you cannot keep everything and everyone you love, and that you cannot avoid the things you do not enjoy, the closer you are to the end of suffering.

It is not just good times and bad times that will pass; we will too. It is useful to work with the phrase, "We too shall pass." "I, too, shall pass." "Mom and Dad, too shall pass." "[Beloved friend/partner] too shall pass."

It is not about *whether* you and your loved ones will die. It is about *when* you and your loved ones will die.

Training Level Two: Keep death in mind

You would do well to spend time considering death and thinking that *today* could be your last day. That this could be the last day of someone you love. The purpose of this practice is not to dwell in a place of morbidity but to appreciate the preciousness of the life you have been given. To be born as a human being is a gift. In this lifetime, you can practice the Dharma. After you die, you might lose this opportunity.

You can save yourself a tremendous amount of pain with some preparation. You do not have to walk around obsessed with death; just hold the possibility of death in your thoughts.

Think about death throughout your day. Use death as a meditation device. Consider the phrase, "Today could be my last day." Death is just one of many experiences that make up a life. It is neither good nor bad. It just is.

One way you can make it easier is to accept death as an integral part of life. A way to accept death into your life is to allow yourself to think about it. Don't turn off thoughts about losing others. Don't turn away from people who have experienced loss. Be part of that experience.

Ignoring people who are sick does not make them well. Refusing to acknowledge death does not make you or anyone else immortal. The more you wish to avoid suffering, the harder it will be. And the more you crave or want for the people you love never to have to leave you, the more difficult it will be when they do.

Training Level Three: Practice the Five Contemplations

The Five Contemplations combine a healthy recognition of impermanence with death awareness. Like a good training plan, level three is drawing from the foundation you built for yourself in levels one and two. Most of the Buddhist monks and nuns that I know chant these contemplations every day. Place these contemplations where you will see them and remember to recite them. Please pay attention to these words and the impact they have on you. Use them in your meditation practice.

"There are these five facts that one should reflect on often, whether one is a woman or a man, lay or ordained. Which five?

"'I am subject to aging, have not gone beyond aging.' This is the first fact that one should reflect on often, whether one is a woman or a man, lay or ordained.

"'I am subject to illness, have not gone beyond illness.'...

"'I am subject to death, have not gone beyond death.' . . .

"'I will grow different, separate from all that is dear and appealing to me.' . . .

"'I am the owner of my actions, heir to my actions, born of my actions, related through my actions, and have my actions as my arbitrator. Whatever I do, for good or for evil, to that will I fall heir.'" (AN 5.57)

Training Level Four: Meditate on death

Meditating on your death and the death of your loved ones is beneficial. It is also challenging. That is why this is level four of your training plan.

When my father told me that his lung cancer was terminal, I meditated on his death. Not so much on the actual moment of his death, but on the fact that he would die, I meditated on him being dead and how I would feel about it. I shed many tears, but it helped me to wrap my head around the fact that he was dying. I used the same approach when my husband was dying.

Long before you have a loved one with a terminal diagnosis, you can develop a solid *maraṇasati* or mindfulness of death practice. In the *Satipatthana Sutta* (MN:10), instructions are given on how to contemplate the body as a body that has been disposed of in the charnel grounds. And remember that just as that body has met various stages of decay, so too will your body. Your body is no different from that body in the charnel ground.

The *Kāyagatāsati Sutta* (MN 119) teaches mindfulness of the body and again refers to charnel ground contemplation to remind us of the impermanence and dissolution we all face.

The *Maraṇasati Sutta* emphasizes the importance of the mindfulness of death. Not just because it makes it easier for us to deal with death, but because it reminds us to be more dedicated to our spiritual practice.

These are not hidden teachings; they are commonly taught in many parts of the world, yet they could be new to you. And if that is the case, remember to seek out a qualified teacher and practice with your local Buddhist community.

Take this training plan and give it a try. Make adjustments that will make it more useful for you. Note that I did not say make adjustments that will make it easier for you. You do not run a successful marathon based on a series of easy sprints.

And know that each time you encounter death, your experience will be a bit different. And if you approach each death from a place of openness, you will improve your practice. You will become stronger. Please remember to keep up with your training. You are not finished until your last race is run.

MARAṆASATI
IS FOR ALL OF US

In the *Maraṇasati Sutta* (AN 6.19), the Buddha calls his monks together and says to them:

"*Mindfulness of death, when developed and pursued, is of great fruit and great benefit. It gains a footing in the Deathless, has the Deathless as its final end. Therefore, you should develop mindfulness of death.*"

Next, some of the monks speak up and describe the various ways in which they are practicing mindfulness of death. One is contemplating that he might just live for a night and a day, another that he might live for just a day, another for the duration of his meal, one to at least chew four morsels of food, and still one more thinking to last just long enough to chew a single bite. Yet a different monk expresses his mindfulness of death by contemplating just one breath.

After listening to these replies, the Buddha instructs all of them:

"*Whoever develops mindfulness of death, thinking, 'O, that I might live for a day and night . . . for a day . . . for the interval that it takes to eat a meal . . . for the interval that it takes to swallow having chewed up four morsels of food, that I might attend to the Blessed One's instructions. I would have accomplished a great deal'—they are said to dwell heedlessly. They develop mindfulness of death slowly for the sake of ending the effluents.*

"But whoever develops mindfulness of death, thinking, 'O, that I might live for the interval that it takes to swallow having chewed up one morsel of food . . . for the interval that it takes to breathe out after breathing in, or to breathe in after breathing out, that I might attend to the Blessed One's instructions. I would have accomplished a great deal'—they are said to dwell heedfully. They develop mindfulness of death acutely for the sake of ending the effluents.

This entire discussion takes place between the Buddha and his monks. Many important teachings from the Pāli Canon take place between the Buddha and his monks. And this has led more than one person to ask me: "Are these teachings relevant to laypeople?" There are definitely times when the Buddha was teaching specifically to his monastics. The *Vinaya* is a good example. And there are teachings that he gave to laypeople. The *Sigālovāda Sutta* is one of the most common examples of a discourse that is specifically meant for laypeople.

When the Buddha taught and only his monks were present, does that mean that laypeople need not be concerned with these teachings? If these lessons were only for the monastic community, why then did his monastics travel and share the teaching that they had committed to memory? With all of the collaboration and agreements that came from the early councils, if these lessons were not meant to be shared, it seems that there would have been stricter controls around keeping the teachings secret or definitively segregating monastic teachings from teachings for the laity.

The Buddha taught suffering and the liberation from suffering. We are all going to die, we will all benefit from having a peaceful death. And to be born into the human realm is a rare gift, not to be squandered. And to me, this means that, yes, we can all access the teachings of *maraṇasati*.

If you find it overwhelming to contemplate that you might die during your meal, start small. You do not have to immediately go right to "I am going to die!" Although some of you might.

Many of us, can benefit from truly reflecting upon the truth that there is suffering and the source of that suffering. Start by considering the Four Noble Truths. We suffer, and the source of that suffering is known wanting things, people, and outcomes. And also, aversion to certain things, or people, or outcomes.

Now consider impermanence. Things are always changing. And the more we hang on to perceptions of how things must be, the more difficult our lives become. You can start by looking at your plans for the day. Sometimes things go exactly as you imagined, and other times the entire day is a disaster. Or is it? When our plans fall apart, we are presented with an opportunity to embrace impermanence.

Those broken plans are a representation of death. Something you relied upon goes away. An assumption becomes invalid, a cherished thing breaks, a relationship ends. Pay attention to your emotions as you watch your plans die. Pay attention to your emotions as you begin to watch your plans die, with acceptance. As you begin to become comfortable with how uncertainty is always a part of your daily life, you can begin to project beyond your daily plans.

The plans you have made for your week, your month, your year—all of this is built on a perception of control and an illusion of certainty. Yet plans help us navigate our lives. Keep making plans, and as you do, acknowledge that there will be impermanence. Some of your plans, or elements of your plans, will die. And when this happens, call it death. Remind yourself that this is a type of death. Now, you are living with death.

As soon as you can, move from the death of things and ideas to the recognition that you and your loved ones are also subject to impermanence. Allow yourself to entertain the thought, "One day I will die." Or "Today could be my last day." Bring these thoughts to your meditation and notice how it feels. Be aware of the emotions that arise, and work to study those emotions. Try to be nonjudgmental. You think what you think, you feel what you feel. Just be with it. Consider reading and chanting the Five Recollections each day. As you spend time following impermanence all the way through a natural progression from plans that died to your death, and the death of your loved ones, eventually, you will develop more ease.

Five Recollections (AN 5.57)

1. I am of the nature to grow old; I am not exempt from aging.

2. I am of the nature to become diseased; I am not exempt from disease.

3. I am of the nature to die; I am not exempt from death.

4. All that is mine, dear, and delightful will change and vanish.

5. I am the owner of my karma; I am born of my karma; I live supported by my karma; I will inherit my karma; whatever I do, whether good or evil, that I will inherit.

Now you are ready to consider that you might chew one more bite, but you also might not chew one more bite.

NINE SIMPLE
WAYS TO CONTEMPLATE DEATH

In the *Abhaya Sutta* (AN 4.84), a Brahman named Janussonin tells the Buddha that he believes that everyone subject to death is terrified of death. He does not believe that anyone can face death without fear. The Buddha agrees that some are afraid of death. And there are those who do not live in terror of death. And then he teaches the difference between those who have conquered their fear of death and those who have not. Spoiler alert: clinging, craving, unskillful actions, and doubting the teachings lead to fearful deaths. Abandoning clinging, living a life of good deeds, and trusting in the Dhamma are the way to a peaceful death.

The Buddha teaches mindfulness of death in the *Maranasati Sutta* (AN 6.19). In the *Satipatthana Sutta* (MN 10), he used charnel ground contemplation to remind monks that their bodies are subject to break up and dissolution and therefore, clinging to the body is to be avoided. These are not light teachings. Nor should they be.

Getting to the point where you can mindfully acknowledge that death can arrive before you finish reading this sentence takes effort. You know it is worth it.

"The perception of death, when developed and pursued, is of great fruit, of great benefit. It gains a footing in the Deathless, has the Deathless as its final end:" Thus, was it said, and in reference to this was it said. (AN 7.46)

If you are like me, some days a deep dive into the suttas is not within reach. Or you might benefit from other ways to become comfortable with death. It can be helpful to spend time understanding the beliefs that you hold about death and dying. And to notice the emotions that surface for you when you contemplate death.

Here are nine thoughts about death. You can use them as mantras, as an object for meditation, or as a way to start thoughtful discussions with family or friends. I invite you to examine this list and to add to it or subtract from it in a way that supports you in your own practice.

1. *Death is inescapable.* You *know* this intellectually. Do you know it as part of your inner wisdom? Can you reflect upon this and remain undisturbed? You know, one plus one is two, everyone dies, two plus two is four, I will also die. Each of these phrases are fact, but even if you dislike math, the phrases everyone dies, and I will also die are probably the phrases that make you feel uncomfortable.

2. *Death can seem capricious.* When your 100-year-old grandmother dies, you can easily make sense of it. But there is also the newborn baby or the new father who stepped into the wrong intersection. There will be death, and beyond knowing that all living creatures die, it may defy logic or your sense of fairness. Stop expecting logic and fairness. Remember that each living being has karma.

3. *Death is normal.* Breathing is a normal bodily function, and it is also normal to eventually stop breathing. This does not mean it is to be trivialized. Normal does not mean insignificant. The death of someone

you love is impactful. And the good news is that since death is not unheard of, you live in a world where there are medical, financial, emotional, and spiritual support systems in place to guide you.

4. *Death is an integral part of life.* Humans have many different milestones. And most of them are recognized and celebrated. In most cultures, we help children prepare to become adults, and we help adults develop to raise children. Sometimes, we help prepare one another to become elderly. But too often, we leave out the discussion and preparation for death. Which is why so many people are surprised by death.

5. *Death is like a snowflake.* No two are exactly alike. Every death is precious and unique. There is so much that we do not see. Most of the time, we see the exterior result: a heart stops beating, the breath becomes still. But every person has a unique final moment. Your ability to help someone experience peace during his or her last moment is invaluable.

6. *Life is precious, and so is death.* Those who live with an acceptance of death die with fewer regrets. Death teaches us to stop wasting time. Death teaches us not to become caught up in petty squabbles.

7. *Death is not evil.* Consider this an invitation to practice equanimity. Starting with this short declaration is a big step.

8. *There is more than one way to celebrate a life.* This is not the time for you and your family to argue over prayers, songs, and memorial services. Just be flexible and celebrate your loved one in the best way possible.

9. *Everyone grieves differently.* Practice being non-judgmental. I have seen loving, crying, praying, laughing, and so much more. The best advice? Don't harm yourself or others. Be patient and practice self-compassion. ***Even those who prepare for death will experience grief.***

The goal is that by contemplating these ideas, you become less fearful and more comfortable. As you go through the list, notice your initial reactions to each of them. What surfaces? Do you feel resistance, anger, fear, sadness, or something else? What is going on in your body? You might even do some journaling, writing your responses to the statements that elicit your strongest feelings, and capturing why some of the statements are easy for you to process.

Each day, you can work to develop and pursue your perception of death. Some days, you will have the time and energy to enter a deep mindfulness of death practice. When that is not possible for you, work with thoughts like the list provided here to continue growing and to make your death practice even more accessible.

SOOTHING THE FEAR OF DEATH: LESSONS FROM NAKULA'S MOTHER

My parents had a family friend who was terminally ill. As his time of death drew closer, his wife suspected that he was having a hard time letting go. He had many siblings. And some of them were able to be by his side during the dying process. But some were not. His wife realized that maybe what he needed was to say goodbye. She called each of the missing siblings and put the phone up to her husband's ear. Miraculously, she was able to get everyone on the phone on the first try. And just a few minutes after he finished the last phone call, her husband took his last breath and died peacefully.

Many people fear leaving behind unfinished business, unfulfilled dreams, or unresolved conflicts with loved ones when they die. They may also worry about the impact that their death will have on their loved ones, such as leaving them with financial burdens or emotional distress.

Those who have loved ones who can help alleviate their fears are fortunate. We see such an example in the *sutta* about Nakula's parents (AN 6.16):

At that time, Nakula's father, the householder, was diseased, in pain, severely ill. Then Nakula's mother said to him: "Don't be worried as you die, householder. Death is painful for one who is worried. The Blessed One has criticized being worried at the time of death.

Now it may be that you are thinking, 'Nakula's mother will not be able to support the children or maintain the household after I'm gone,' but you shouldn't see things in that way. I am skilled at spinning cotton, at carding matted wool. I can support the children and maintain the household after you are gone. So don't be worried as you die, householder. Death is painful for one who is worried. The Blessed One has criticized being worried at the time of death.

Now it may be that you are thinking, 'Nakula's mother will take another husband after I'm gone,' but you shouldn't see things in that way. You know as well as I how my fidelity has been constant for the past sixteen years. So don't be worried as you die, householder. Death is painful for one who is worried. The Blessed One has criticized death when one is worried.

Now it may be that you are thinking, 'Nakula's mother will have no desire to go see the Blessed One, to go see the community of monks, after I'm gone,' but you shouldn't see things in that way. I will have an even greater desire to go see the Blessed One, to go see the community of monks, after you are gone. So don't be worried as you die, householder. Death is painful for one who is worried. The Blessed One has criticized being worried at the time of death.

The *sutta* goes on to discuss fears that Nakula's mother will not live according to the precepts, or that she will not attain inner tranquility of awareness, or that she does not gain a firm foothold in the Dhamma. And with each fear, Nakula's mother assures her dying husband that his fears will not come true. In this story, her husband recovers. And after his recovery, he visits the Buddha, who tells him that it is to his great gain that he has Nakula's mother to guide him.

I remember that as my father was dying, he was worried about my mother. A discussion we had always was that when either of them died, the survivor would come to live with me and my husband. If not actually in our house with us, then in the area. The idea being that my husband and I were still working, and it would be difficult for us to travel two states away to take care of the survivor. But when the time came, my mother was not going to do this. She did not want to come live with us or near us; she wanted to stay in the house that she and my father had lived in, and she wanted to maintain her independence. When my father told me about her decision, he was concerned about her well-being and her financial position. At that point, we had been making monthly trips to their area to be with them through Dad's final days. I assured him that if Mom wanted to stay, we were fully prepared to support her, whatever that meant. And I meant it, and he knew that I meant it, and he was relieved. As he moved closer to breathing his final breath, we continued to assure him that Mom would be well taken care of.

My mother did not go through a terminal illness, but a day before she died of a heart attack, she expressed concerns about my well-being—she knew that my husband was terminally ill and she worried about what my future would look like. And I did not give her false hope, but I did let her know that I was as well-positioned as possible for his pending death.

When someone you love is dying, you can provide a peaceful environment by being with them and supporting their journey. Like Nakula's mother, you can give assurances and help to alleviate their fears by allowing them the freedom to let go and proceed with the transition.

For yourself, travel lightly! Good advice for vacations and other adventures, and a way to live. Be aware of what you are carrying around with you and your willingness to let go. Live well, meaning follow the Noble Eightfold Path. When you don't live well, or if you have unresolved issues, do what you need to do to find peace. In that way, when it is your time, you will have less clinging and less aversion.

OUR PETS, OUR TEACHERS

"I never want to have another dog again." The woman sitting next to me was adamant. I was a bit surprised at the strength of her declaration. First, because we did not know one another, and second, because we live in a very pet-centric society. It was an interesting declaration to make in a neighborhood where many shops and restaurants have water bowls and treats at the ready for the steady stream of dogs who walk by with their humans.

"It is too hard," she continued. "You get to know them, you learn to love them, and then they die. I don't think I can say goodbye to one more dog." And then I began to understand her perspective. In a world where we might keep physical and emotional distance from other human beings, many of us have become increasingly attached to our pets. Our dogs, cats, birds, fish, and reptiles have become friends and family members. In short, many people develop deep attachments to their animal companions. And the grief that comes with loss when this attachment is broken is intense. The choice that this woman was making was not to engage. To love a sentient being without attachment is difficult. This is why you can find various quotes that associate grief as part of love, or grief as the price of love.

In most cases, to love a pet is to know that you will outlive that pet. When interviewing teachers for my book *Sitting with Death: Buddhist Insights to Help You Face Your Fears and Live a Peaceful Life,* many of the teachers shared that their first experiences with death came from childhood and the death of a family pet. To live with a pet is to observe the cycle of aging and death. I have had the benefit of being part of this journey with more than one cat. A cat named Alex, really taught me about aging.

Her longevity amazed me. When her companion cat died, Alex went through a very rough patch. She lost weight, and her fur fell out. She was grieving. I began to realize that she, too, would soon be gone. Soon actually became two-and-a-half years later. And during that time, I began to look on her as my aging coach or mentor. She was showing me what it was like to be an old lady. Watching her experience the challenges of aging, I was amazed at the grace and dignity with which she navigated her days. Somedays, she would look at me as if to say, "Can you believe this?" But she forged ahead, making every day her own and teaching me valuable lessons as she did so.

As she aged, Alex either ate or she did not. Some days nothing would entice her to eat. One evening, she practically assaulted one of my friends over a cupcake. It's about the balance between extremes. I do not recall too many days when she snacked. The good news was that until her last week, the not-eating versus the eating remained in balance. I recall watching my mother-in-law go through something very similar. Some days, she would tell me that everything was too salty. Other days, she would clean her plate and reach across to finish mine. Her weight was consistent until the week before she died.

Alex never knew herself to be anything other than a pretty cat. Even when her fur fell out and she had a bald stripe down her back, I told her she was a pretty girl. And she would look at me, blink, and rub her head against my hand. No matter how old you get, and how much your looks may change, to someone you will be beautiful. Accept compliments and affection with grace. Let friends and loved ones shower you with hugs and compliments. It's good for all of you.

Logically, we know that things are going to change. Parts of your body will work differently or not at all. At some point, Alex lost her hearing. I don't know exactly when it happened. I discovered it after her companion cat died. One day, Alex just started screaming, and as much as I called to her, she did not respond. I realized that she had relied on her companion cat as her hearing guide. Eventually, we both adjusted. I learned that if I needed her attention, I could thump on the floor with my foot, and she would feel the vibrations and respond. She learned that she could meow at me like always, and I would respond. She adapted to her hearing limitation and kept going.

As a young cat, Alex loved to go outdoors. She had no intention of becoming an indoor cat. In the last couple of years, she would go next door to eat the neighbor's grass, do a lap around her yard, and then come in. In her last year, she would eat the neighbor's grass, come back, lie in the sun, and then come in. In her last few weeks, she would go outside, sniff the air, lie down in the sun, and come back in within 10 minutes. You too should seek to continue to enjoy fresh air and sunlight and good company and beautiful art, and music that brings you joy for as long as you can. You could lament the fact that you can no longer run a 10k, or you can get out and walk up and down the sidewalk. Or sit in the front yard. The choice is yours; the clock is ticking.

As Alex aged, she needed digestive aids, special medicine, and more than one type of special food. She drank lactose-free milk. She did not always hit the litter box. And she had no problem waking me up to let me know that she needed something. None of this gave her any concern. And it should not bother you either. You are here, and you are doing your best.

Live your life to the fullest and make every moment count.

On more than one occasion, I thought that Alex was at death's door. She rallied several times. I joked with friends that the Grim Reaper would come, Alex would start to follow him, and then she would stop and say, "Hey, wait a minute, I am a cat. I have nine lives. Read the contract, buddy. It's not time yet." You and I do not have nine lives, but we do have the ability to maximize our time. Live until you have no more life left to live. And if you decide to share that life with a pet, let that pet become part of your practice. To learn how to love without (or with less) attachment, to learn how to age, and how to live until you die.

References

Meloni, Margaret. Sitting with Death: *Buddhist Insights to Help You Face Your Fears and Live a Peaceful Life. Long Beach*, CA: Meloni Coaching Solutions.

THE ART OF CARING: EMBRACING THE JOURNEY OF PROVIDING LOVE WITHOUT EXPECTATIONS

One day, you may find yourself caring for a sick family member. And while it's natural to hope for the best and to become attached to a specific outcome, the truth is that your role is about being present in the moment and offering support without conditions. In helping out your elder, your ill family member, or your dying loved one, you have been handed an opportunity to work with non-attachment and impermanence. What a relief that you have access to mindfulness and compassion!

If you come from a goal-oriented culture. You might jump into this challenge with both feet. If you are going to be a caretaker, then you will be the best, the most loving, the most caring. You will work miracles. Depending on the situation, having an objective for the day might be helpful. Or it can lead both of you to feel frustrated. If someone is terminally ill, you are providing comfort. If someone is on the way to recovery, you are providing help on the path to improvement—in this case, you want to strike a balance between striving for improvement and providing unconditional love and support.

This is neither the time nor the place to assess yourself in terms of success or failure.

As a caregiver, it's natural to want to see progress in your loved one's condition, but this desire should not become the sole focus of your caregiving journey. Realize that every circumstance is different, and that progress may take time or may look different from what you originally envisioned. And progress for someone who is dying is very different than progress for someone who is recovering. Your one true goal is to remember that your loved one's well-being is the priority. What you definitely *can* do is be human and do the best that you can do in the circumstances presented to you. And trust me, when you are caring for someone who is ailing, that is significant.

If, at the end of the day, the one you care for has an improvement, do not count this as your success. If, at the end of the day, the one you care for is worse, do not count this as your failure. You do not force outcomes. Try to accept the situation as it is. Right now, it is like this. You are there, and you are providing care, and you are doing the best you can. You are providing emotional support as well as you can and performing the appropriate tasks. You don't need to give yourself a performance appraisal. Just provide care for the sake of providing care. For the love of your person, for compassion's sake.

The time spent together and the bond you build with your loved one are invaluable. A simple gesture or a shared moment of laughter can become a treasured memory that serves as a reminder of the love and dedication you are providing in your caregiving journey. Your efforts enhance your loved one's quality of life in countless small ways, so view each task as an opportunity to express your love and support. By approaching your role with gratitude and mindfulness, you can maintain a sense of purpose and fulfillment in your caregiving journey.

Each day, and even each moment of each day, everything is changing. Impermanence is at play. To think that you will be able to control the conditions that you and your loved ones will face during your caretaking is ridiculous. There are no certainties. When faced with death or serious illness, it's natural to worry about what the future may hold and to search for answers or reassurances.

You might find yourself wondering, "What will happen tomorrow, or this afternoon, or in the next moment?" Your role does call for some proactive measures—for example, keeping important prescriptions filled and available. However, you cannot predict or control the future.

Let mindfulness be your guide. Focus on taking things one day at a time. This allows you to stay present in the moment and to navigate each new challenge as it arises.

It's human nature to try to prepare for the worst-case scenario, and your imagination can get the best of you. You may start worrying about all sorts of problems and complications. It is wise to be prepared and well-informed but just do not become caught up in hypothetical situations.

Instead of worrying about what *might* happen, focus on the situation at hand. Address the needs and concerns of your loved one and yourself as they arise, rather than getting lost in a sea of "what-ifs." By staying present and focused on the reality of the situation, you'll be better equipped to provide the care and support your loved one needs.

In truth, there is so much that you do not know. And if you can welcome a sense of comfort with the unknown, you can save yourself so much suffering. Be with what is happening *now*. You do not need to envision future pain and problems and sit with those right now. You do not know what will come, how it will come, or when it will come. Practice your non-attachment to outcomes, your mindfulness, and your compassion toward yourself and others, and you will build the resilience you need for whatever comes next.

NOBODY GETS
OUT OF THIS ALIVE

Some do not understand
that we must die,
But those who do realize this
settle their quarrels. (Dhp verse 6)

"Nobody gets out of this alive." This is what my father said when faced with his diagnosis of terminal lung cancer. It was not his original saying, but it fit the situation and his personality. I have to think that, when faced with his mortality, Dad must have had some complicated and conflicting thoughts. But with us, he was always steady. Always the stoic New Englander. He wanted to make sure that we understood that he was dying. Not in any dramatic, morbid sense. He just wanted to know that we were in tune with reality. If he could not live, he was going to try to help us face his death. And with his strength, his faith, and his compassion for us, he helped us prepare for his death.

There was only one time when he indulged in a little bit of cynicism. And even that made sense. We had always shared a similar sense of humor. We loved puns, we enjoyed a dry wit, and sometimes a hint of sarcasm. So, when one of the nurses at the oncology center was reviewing his medications with him and asked him what they did for him, for just a brief moment, Dad looked at me, cracked a wry smile, and said so quietly that I think only I could hear him, "Apparently nothing." Truer words were never spoken. The blood pressure medication and the cholesterol medication did nothing to ward off the lung cancer.

Those who have come to be,
those who will be:
All
will go,
leaving the body behind.
The skillful person,
realizing the loss of all,
should live the holy life ardently. (Ud 5.2)

In facing his death, my father relied upon his faith. He was a devout Catholic. It was his community that helped him remain mentally strong as his time drew near. He never forced his beliefs on me. He would occasionally discuss how his faith was helping him, as a way of letting me know that he was not afraid to die.

Aside from saying, "Nobody gets out of this alive," Dad would also say, "I never ask why me—really, the question is why not me?"

Where his Catholicism helped him, Buddhism helped me. Developing an understanding of karma, impermanence, and death led me to a similar place. I would never ask, "Why does Dad have to die?" I knew that he, like all of us, was subject to old age, illness, and death.

For before long, how sad! This body will lie upon the ground, cast aside, devoid of consciousness, like a useless charred log.(Dhp verse 41)

As part of his treatment, Dad received radiation. Not because it was going to cure his cancer, but because it could minimize a painful tumor on his back. We made a family outing of his first visit to the oncology center.

The staff at the center were warm and loving. They were happy to see family members in attendance. They wanted to see family members participating in the treatment process.

The technician for the TrueBeam radiation machine was happy to invite us in and give us a tour. He showed us how the device worked and how the beam rotated around the body. He let us stay while he worked to position Dad. He was happy to share his work and glad to see a family involved. But he also understood the reality of Dad's cancer, and he knew that he was helping to alleviate pain, not curing cancer. We left the room when it was time for the actual treatment to begin. I was trying to be cheerful and nonchalant, tugging on Dad's toes as I walked past him, but I was fighting back my tears, and so was the technician.

Those radiation treatments did shrink the tumor and did quite a bit to reduce Dad's pain. One day, during a visit after his radiation treatments ended, Dad sat me down at his computer and asked me to show him how to create a decorative certificate using Word. I was a bit surprised because in the past, he had made fun and silly certificates and sent them to me. "Best Daughter to Watch *Godzilla* With" was one of my favorites. I was his only daughter, but I took the win!

Later, I would realize that the point was to create the certificate together. To spend time on an activity that was part of his cancer, but not in a negative way. He wanted us to have a special and fun memory from this experience. Together, we created a certificate for "Trudy," the name that he gave to the TrueBeam radiation machine. He gave one copy to me, one to the team, and the technician at the oncology center. They loved it. After he died, one of them approached me to let me know that they kept the certificate in the radiation room. It made everybody smile.

Nobody gets out of this alive, but we can live as fully as possible and benefit the lives of others until our final day draws near.

Chapter 2

Rebirth, Karma, and Letting Go

———•———

Welcome to an exploration of rebirth and karma—a gentle invitation for you to pause, ponder, and perhaps see the world (and yourself) with fresh eyes. In this section, you'll dive into the heart of Buddhist teachings on how your intentions, actions, and patterns of mind create your future.

Here, you'll find thought-provoking essays and reflections that unpack common misunderstandings of rebirth and karma. Rather than dry doctrine, these pieces aim to spark your curiosity, inviting you to question long-held assumptions and to discover the deeper meaning that lies beneath. Each article offers a chance to consider:

- How misconceptions of rebirth can lead you into unskillful coping habits—like clinging to fleeting comforts or avoiding responsibility—and how a clearer view can open the door to wiser choices.

- Why the principle of karma is really an invitation to wake up to ethical responsibility, reminding you that every kind thought, word, and deed travels onward and leaves its mark.

- How practicing compassionate detachment—gently releasing your grasp even on those you love—can become one of the most caring acts of all, aligning your heart with freedom rather than fear.

As you read, you might notice familiar ideas stirring in new ways, or you may uncover new questions. Perhaps you'll find a fresh perspective on loss, change, or your longings. These writings encourage a spirit of open inquiry—because in Buddhism, the path to wisdom begins not with blind faith, but with honest reflection. May this journey through rebirth and karma awaken your capacity for kindness, wonder, and mindful engagement with every moment.

PLEASE DON'T COME BACK

For a brief period in the early nineties, I had a job where I did a considerable amount of travel. When I took the position, I knew there would be travel. I could expect to be away one week per month. Technically, this was correct. By the time I left the position, my average travel time was one week per month. But most months, I was gone three weeks per month, followed by some months with very little travel. After the novelty of expense accounts and fancy dinners wore off, I realized how much I missed my friends and family. One morning, while on the road, I awoke from a bad dream. I dreamed that I had come home, only to learn that one of my closest friends had moved away. In my dream, I did not know where she had gone and this hurt me to my core.

It was not until several years later that I encountered Buddhism. The concept of *dukkha* or suffering was not easy for me. But one look at my fears over my friend disappearing helped me understand that I had attachment issues. Even now, I can recall how sad and empty I felt when I awoke from that dream. This attachment, coupled with the fact that I believed in past lives as a young child, made it easy for me to accept the concept of rebirth. The idea of rebirth was reassuring to me. Goodbyes were not final. I would probably see you again in the next life or, if not the next, a future one.

I know now that I am guilty of using rebirth to become less afraid of losing the ones I love. Thinking that there was no real goodbye with rebirth, I grew less anxious about saying goodbye to friends who were moving away. The belief that I would be with others again in another life helped me to accept their deaths. This is the wrong view.

As my husband was dying, we occasionally used the concept of rebirth to help us both feel better about our impending separation. My crazy plan was that he should come back as a cat and find me. Then, if he had a nice long cat life when he died, it would probably be about time for me to die, and we would be together again. We both knew this was silly, yet it did help us smile during some rough discussions.

At best, a flawed plan. To come back as a cat is not a desirable rebirth. And if he did come back as a cat, how would he find me? And if he saw me, how would I recognize him? Would I adopt him, or turn my back on him? Maybe I would adopt him, but he would be a "bad" cat, misbehaving and biting me, and trashing my house? We each have this lifetime to move forward with our practice. There are many possible forms of rebirth and no guarantees. To be born a human is rare and is not to be wasted. While some house cats may disagree, rebirth as a human is the path to the end of suffering.

Then the Blessed One, picking up a little bit of dust with the tip of his fingernail, said to the monks, "What do you think, monks? Which is greater: the little bit of dust I have picked up with the tip of my fingernail, or the great Earth?"

"The great Earth is far greater, lord. The little bit of dust the Blessed One has picked up with the tip of his fingernail is next to nothing. It doesn't even count. It's no comparison. It's not even a fraction, this little bit of dust the Blessed One has picked up with the tip of his fingernail, when compared with the great Earth."

"In the same way, monks, few are the beings reborn among human beings. Far more are those reborn elsewhere. Thus you should train yourselves: 'We will live heedfully.' That's how you should train yourselves." (SN 20.2)

The goal is *not* to come back as a cat *or* a human. The goal is *not to come back*. To skillfully apply the right view is not to cling to seeing your loved ones again.

For one who is born
there's death.

One who is born
sees pain.

It's a binding, a flogging, a torment.

That's why one shouldn't approve
of birth.

The Awakened One taught me the Dhamma
—the overcoming of birth—
for the abandoning of all pain,

he established me in
the truth.

But beings who have come to form
& those with a share in the formless,
if they don't discern cessation,
return to becoming-again. (SN 5.6)

Once there is birth, death will follow. It does not have to be true that once there is death, rebirth will follow. To become comfortable with death and to be less attached to life is to advance along the path away from suffering. Do not look at rebirth to bring you comfort; instead, wish that those you love will escape this endless *samsara* of birth, death, and rebirth.

PS. I do not think that either of my cats is my deceased husband, reborn—I promise.

THE PROBLEM WITH GHOSTS

On the pros and cons of seeing our dead loved ones.

One thing was clear: my father was concerned about my mother. He had told me so himself. He approached me while I was chopping vegetables for dinner. He quietly waited for me to notice him, and then he said: "I am worried about your mother." Before I could respond, he disappeared. He was not swift of foot or a magician. He was dead.

When my father vanished, he left me with so many questions. Was Mom OK? Was that my father? Shouldn't he be somewhere else? Did I see him, or was I having a stroke, or suffering from an overactive imagination?

Was Mom OK?

Mom was doing the best she could. At this point, she was physically healthy. I knew from our daily phone calls that she was a little bit in denial about her emotional state. She had lost her loving partner and best friend. They had been married for 54 years. When I think of a couple who were still deeply in love and not together out of habit, my parents were always the first couple to come to mind. Mom came from a time and place when admitting to being depressed was perceived as a weakness. She could, however, admit to a sense of deep sadness. She was not facing an immediate physical or mental health emergency. For our discussion, yes, Mom was OK.

Was I having a stroke?

No. Unless it came and went in a flash, with no lasting side effects, I was not in the midst of a neurological event. And this takes us to:

Did I see my father's ghost?

There is nobody who can back me up on this. When my father's ghost shared his concerns with me, I was in the kitchen by myself. The only one who can vouch for me is my father's ghost. That's awkward. And if you are skeptical, it is very convenient. Maybe I was projecting. Maybe while chopping vegetables, I had been thinking of my parents and how they loved and cared for one another. Perhaps I imagined the entire encounter. This is the most straightforward explanation. Maybe I saw a ghost.

The problem with ghosts

Most religions allow for the existence of ghosts, spirits, and other supernatural beings. We currently do not have definitive scientific evidence for or against the spirit world. A popular theory is that people who identify with a religious belief system are more likely to report seeing ghosts. And the ghosts we see fall in line with the teachings we follow.

My father was a devoted practicing Catholic. If I saw him, then it was because God had allowed him to come back to Earth to deliver his message. But I'm not a Catholic. I'm a Buddhist. We do not share the same beliefs about ghosts and spirits. Was my father following his rules or mine?

Maybe there is a sorting system. After death, we go to a way station, and then we are redirected according to our religion, or lack thereof. I can picture it now: "OK, Buddhists go to holding section three and wait for further instructions. We will need to sort you according to your sect. Catholics, line one is for you. Muslims go to the holding section two and wait for further instructions. Sunnis and Shia do not worry; we will divide you up once you arrive in section two. Jews, please go to holding section one. We understand that all Jews are not alike. You will receive further instructions once you reach section one. If you identify as Christian but NOT Catholic, make your way over to holding section four. We will need to sort you according to your sect. Hindus, holding section five. If you lived in East Asia and we have not listed your belief system, please go to section six. Native peoples, go to section seven. Atheists, line three is for you. If we have *not* called out your religion, please go to the holding section eight. Undecided, pick something NOW."

And then, if any of the deceased wish to make a return visit, he or she goes through a similar sorting system to get their ghost visa. Catholic father visiting a Buddhist daughter, please follow the Vatican guidelines on friendly hauntings.

It's not the problem with ghosts. It's MY problem with ghosts

Any time after I have had conversations with the ghosts of my dead loved ones, I have been hit with remorse. "Why is he/she still here? He/she shouldn't be here helping me. He/she should have moved on."

As a Buddhist, once you go to the holding section three and get sorted into your sect, you follow a path. In my sorting group, you are either reborn or have already conquered suffering, and there is no more rebirth. There is the possibility that one gets lost or is resistant to rebirth.

My problem with ghosts is that, as much as I have enjoyed visits from my father, and later my deceased mother or husband, I do not *want* them to be able to visit me. I wish they had gone beyond suffering. If not beyond suffering, I wish that they had moved on to a quick and beneficial rebirth. If neither of these is true, then they are possibly visiting me as hungry ghosts. And that is a horrible rebirth. It means that my loved one is suffering due to actions he or she committed in his or her previous life. And I do not want to think that the people I loved had karma that brought them back as hungry ghosts. Or as a *deva*, which is better, but still not desirable. Ultimately, the possibility that allows him or her to visit me as a ghost is not the goal.

Now, my problem with ghosts is becoming less about my ghosts and more about my attachments. Aversion is a form of clinging. On the one hand, I want to say I saw my father's ghost. But then, because I'm not too fond of the implications of that, I don't want it to be true.

Maybe none of us has it correct? Or perhaps this is an idea that I cling to because I do not want to view my father as a hungry ghost, a *deva*, or a demon?

RESPONSIBILITY AND REBIRTH

"Some people reject the idea of rebirth because they do not want the responsibility."

Our teacher made this comment quickly and almost as an afterthought. At that moment, I did not give it much consideration. But later, his statement would come back to me, and I began to contemplate his words. Why is the concept of rebirth challenging for some Buddhists? If you start typing a question about Buddhism and rebirth into your favorite search engine, you will see a common theme in your search results:

- Can you be a Buddhist without believing in rebirth?
- Should I believe in rebirth?
- Are there Buddhists who don't believe in rebirth?
- What does Buddhism teach about life after death?

The term reincarnation makes several appearances, too. Understandably so, as some use the terms rebirth and reincarnation interchangeably. Reincarnation relies on the transmigration of a soul. Meaning, the same soul is returning to a different body. Rebirth is the state of being born again, of returning for another life. And in some Buddhist traditions, this may be recognized as a choice, such as in Mahāyāna, where a bodhisattva purposefully delays attaining nirvana in order to help others. Or, more commonly, it can be the result of one's karma and state of mind at the time of death.

The fact that so many people question whether or not belief in rebirth is a requirement demonstrates that this is an element of Buddhism that is challenging for some to accept. The purpose here is not to resolve whether your acceptance or rejection of rebirth qualifies you as a Buddhist. Please choose your labels. Instead, this is a high-level exploration of why rebirth is difficult to accept and what that means in terms of your responsibility for your behavior.

When I have asked some of my colleagues who are Buddhist monks about rebirth, some of them cut me off. Responding with either, "It's OK if you are not ready for rebirth, you can still follow the Buddha's teachings." Or "Rebirth is absolutely a central theme in Buddhism. You better get used to it." When they realize that I want to ask why some people feel challenged by the concept of rebirth, they are usually more candid. It seems that they are accustomed to someone like me, an individual who grew up in a Christian family in a Christian country, taking issue with rebirth. Actually, for as long as I can remember, rebirth always made sense to me. I was an anomaly in my family and my community.

The Pāli Canon references rebirth. Passages such as this one emphasize that the human form is the most fortunate of rebirths and that there are many other forms:

Then the Blessed One, picking up a little bit of dust with the tip of his fingernail, said to the monks, "What do you think, monks? Which is greater: the little bit of dust I have picked up with the tip of my fingernail, or the great Earth?"

"The great Earth is far greater, lord. The little bit of dust the Blessed One has picked up with the tip of his fingernail is next to nothing. It doesn't even count. It's no comparison. It's not even a fraction, this little bit of dust the Blessed One has picked up with the tip of his fingernail when compared with the great Earth."

"In the same way, monks, few are the beings reborn among human beings. Far more are those reborn elsewhere. Thus, you should train yourselves: 'We will live heedfully.' That's how you should train yourselves." (SN 20.2)

For many practitioners of Theravāda Buddhism, accepting that the Buddha taught liberation from suffering and that suffering results in a continuous cycle of death and rebirth is central to understanding the Four Noble Truths and the Noble Eightfold Path.

Some believe that the cycle of rebirth is not mentioned consistently enough throughout the Pāli Canon to be considered part of the path reliably. They are opening the door to skepticism. Others see no need for rebirth to be part of the teachings and part of their practice. The idea of one life might be more motivating than the opportunity to "get it right" across many lifetimes.

If you did not grow up in a community where rebirth was part of your socio-religious experience, the idea of rebirth might seem foreign. It might not fit into your worldview. But this passage, in its direct simplicity, might form the basis of your understanding of Buddhism:

"To avoid all evil, to cultivate good, and to cleanse one's mind—this is the teaching of the Buddhas." (Dhp 183)

Whether you accept rebirth or not, you are responsible for your actions and the results of your actions. The above passage does not say to have someone else cleanse your mind. *You* are to avoid evil and to foster good.

This excerpt states that you are responsible for the results of your actions:

"Student beings are owners of karma, heir to karma, born of karma, related through karma, and have karma as their arbitrator. Karma is what creates distinctions among beings in terms of coarseness & refinement." (MN 135)

The passage goes on to describe in detail unskillful actions, such as killing, stealing, and lack of generosity, and more. It also describes the results of unskillful behavior, and those results mention rebirth. Within these teachings, it becomes clear: *you* are the master of your outcome. Your actions, wholesome or otherwise, are what shape what happens next. And while some may see this as freeing. Others may feel the heaviness of responsibility. Maybe worrying about one lifetime full of actions is enough to bear. At the end of one lifetime, one outcome seems more manageable—just one finish line to cross without worrying about the next one. Whether you accept rebirth or not, your result is in your hands. Your freedom from suffering is *your* responsibility.

REBIRTH AND RIGHT VIEW: A PERSONAL JOURNEY

It's no problem to say goodbye to someone because rebirth teaches us that we will be together again anyway, right? Wrong, as in that's the wrong view! I carried that view around for a few years. This view was a crutch, a coping mechanism to help me process the painful emotions that came from being apart from people who were important to me.

Unlike some of my other Buddhist friends from a Judeo-Christian background, I did not have a problem accepting the idea of rebirth. My belief in rebirth made it easier for me to become a Buddhist. I recall that since I was a child, the concept of rebirth made sense to me. I have no idea why. Once, when I spoke about it with my mother, she was just as baffled. There had not been any encounters in our family or our community with Hindus or Buddhists. My belief was just a part of who I was.

When I began to learn about Buddhism, I spent time contemplating rebirth. Sitting with different Buddhist groups and learning from multiple teachers exposed me to ideas such as:

- At one point, everyone has been your mother

- Or you were their mother

- Or both

Other teachings focused on the idea that we have all been in each other's lives in different ways, across many lifetimes. Or people with whom you've had difficulties keep popping up in your various lifetimes until these issues resolve. A classmate and I started out with a combative relationship and began to joke that he had killed me in another lifetime. I do not know how we got to this point, but we did. After a while, he no longer enjoyed the joke because the idea of it being true upset him. When I understood that this was no longer funny to him, I stopped kidding with him about poisonings and stabbings and shootings. We just became friends.

At some point, I began to use the idea of rebirth as a way to console myself when I knew I might not see someone again. This made it easier for me when friends moved far away, or a colleague I enjoyed left the company, or a classmate I liked moved on. As a form of defense, or in response to the attachment I had for that person, I would remind myself that they were leaving now, but I would probably see them again in another life. For the most part, that helped me feel less sad.

This approach was helpful to me. As I moved forward with my Buddhist practice, and I wrote about my experiences in losing my key family members, and I interviewed Buddhist teachers about their experiences with death and grief, I began to see the error of my ways.

In a discussion with my teacher, I asked: "Is it better to celebrate death and be sad about birth?" I expected him to validate me and tell me that I was correct. Instead, he gently told me that when someone dies, you do not know what his/her/their rebirth will be. What if this person is reborn in a lesser realm? He taught me that the best wish for others is that they do not return at all.

This brief but significant exchange paved the way for me to reconsider my dependence on rebirth to avoid the pain of separation. I should not use the idea of rebirth to feel better about someone leaving my life. This idea of hoping to see someone again in another lifetime is selfish. I began to understand my thoughts on rebirth as a form of arrested development. Instead of sitting with my feelings of loss and abandonment, I was trying to block those feelings. There was no need to process any sadness, I could just put it all on hold—I was going to see my friend again. Probably not for many years, and without memories of this lifetime together, but it would happen. And how did that work out for me? It didn't stop me from feeling sad or from missing the people who had moved on. It simply blocked me from doing the necessary work in my practice.

I should not want any of us to be together in a future life; the goal is to experience liberation from suffering and to stop returning. I do not want to lean on rebirth as a crutch. I do not want the idea of future lives to prevent me from working with my attachment to others. It's time to put down the crutch and keep walking on the path.

MATTERS OF METTĀ AND MERIT

You sit down to meditate and engage in *mettā* practice. You develop feelings of goodwill toward others and seek to establish a mind free of ill will. As you complete your meditation, you dedicate your merit so that all beings may be free of suffering. You might wonder, if you have already generated thoughts of goodwill toward others, whether sending merit is an unnecessary extra? *Mettā* and merit work together. You might find it helpful to think of them as part of the same system

Some translate *mettā* as loving-kindness; others prefer the phrase goodwill. For our discussion, let's think of it as the ability to direct well-wishes to others. To sincerely want others to be well and happy. Merit is a force that comes from the good deeds you have done, assuming that you committed those good deeds with the right intention. It is bound to our *kamma*. Our actions, past and present, shape our experience in this life and in the next. To practice good deeds with the right intention requires a mind free of ill will.

Mettā allows you to behave in a way that supports the creation of merit. As you move forward with your *mettā* practice, you can direct well-wishes to an expanding circle of beings. So that when you say, "May all beings be happy and free from suffering." You mean *all* beings. Difficult friends, family, and coworkers included. And now, you have created or added to your merit store. This passage from the *Itivuttaka* sheds some light on *mettā* and merit together:

Train in acts of merit
that bring long-lasting bliss—
develop giving,
a life in tune,
a mind of goodwill.
Developing these
three things
that bring about bliss,
the wise reappear
in a world of bliss
unalloyed.
(Iti 1.22)

A mind of goodwill is an important component of merit. As taught in the Pāli canon, merit comes from three sources: generosity (*dāna*), virtue (*sīla*), and mental development (*bhāvana*). *Mettā-bhāvana* is not the only way that you collect merit; in fact, of the 10 ways to generate merit, *dāna* is the most significant. But *mettā* makes it possible for you to become capable of creating merit and of benefiting from merit that you have earned in past lives.

This passage from *Mettā: The Philosophy and Practice of Universal Love* by Acharya Buddharakkhita explains the critical role that *mettā* plays in helping us receive the power of our merit:

When one projects this total wish for others to dwell happily, free from hostility, affliction and distress, not only does one elevate oneself to a level where true happiness prevails, but one sets in motion powerful vibrations conducive to happiness, cooling off enmity, relieving affliction and distress. (Buddharakkhita 1989)

Mettā has been identified as that specific factor which "ripens" the accumulated merit *(puñña)* acquired by the 10 ways for the acquisition of merit *(dasapunna-kiriyavatthu),* such as the practice of generosity, virtue, and so on. Again, it *is mettā* that brings to maturity the 10 exalted spiritual qualities known as "perfections" *(pāramitā).*

The human mind is like a mine holding an inexhaustible storehouse of spiritual power and insight. This immense inner potential of merit can be fully exploited only by the practice of *mettā*, as is clear from the description of *mettā* as that "maturing force" which ripens the dormant merits. In the *Maṅgala Sutta*, it is said that only after one has achieved an elevating interpersonal relationship (by resorting to good company, and so on) does one choose the right environment for the merits of the past to find fruition. This finding of fruition is exactly what *mettā* does. Mere avoidance of wrong company and living in a cultured environment is not enough; the mind must be cultivated by *mettā*. Hence the allusion to the fruition of past merit.

At this point, you might be wondering, what does this have to do with *Death Dhamma*? Merit earned in this life follows you to the next. Consider the final statement in this passage from the *Saṃyutta Nikāya*:

Grain, wealth, silver, gold,
or whatever other belongings you have;
slaves, servants, errand-runners,
& any dependents:
you must go without taking
any of them;
you must leave
all of them
behind.

What you do
with body, speech, or mind:
that is yours;
taking
that you go;
that's
your follower,
like a shadow
that never leaves.

Thus you should do what is fine
as a stash for the next life.
Acts of merit
are the support for beings
in their after-death world. (SN 3.20)

Not only does your merit help you, but you can also use it to help your deceased loved ones. You can transfer the merit you earn. We use *mettā*, sending well-wishes to other living beings, and when we can develop this state of goodwill toward others, we ripen the merit we have been carrying, and we are more likely to behave in ways that will add to our merit store. We can then dedicate our merit to our deceased family. We cannot do anything about the fact that they have died. We cannot control *if* they are reborn or *when* or *where* they are reborn. We can send them merit and, if the conditions are right, your merit will benefit them. When you can channel the energy of your grief into doing good deeds for others or sending your compassionate thoughts to others, you are creating positive energy, and the deceased may benefit from that energy.

Take note of this qualifier: "if the conditions are right." The *Janussonin Sutta* discusses offerings to the dead. Janussonin is a Brahmin who asks the Buddha about the conditions under which the dead may receive gifts from the living. Merit is the gift. The Buddha teaches Janussonin that merit only reaches those who are in what he refers to as the possible places, but not those who are in the impossible places. The list of impossible places includes the hell realm, the animal realm, the human realm, and the deva world. The possible place? The realm of hungry ghosts. Your merit reaches your dead family members who have become hungry ghosts.

With more impossible places than possible places, Janussonin wonders what will happen if none of his ancestors are hungry ghosts? The Buddha assures Janussonin that it is likely that there will be an ancestor on hand to receive the merit. In the rare instance that there is not, the donor still receives the benefits that come from seeking to transfer merit to others. The *sutta* goes on to discuss how one who otherwise would have a less than desirable rebirth can avoid landing in one of the impossible places. The response is generosity. Generosity in this life creates merit. Transferring or dedicating your merit to others is an act of giving that helps you, and possibly your ancestors. And you are inspired to give when you are free of animosity, when you have a mind of goodwill.

References

Buddharakkhita, Acariya. 1989. *Mettā: The Philosophy and Practice of Universal Love*. Kandy: Buddhist Publication Society.

Chapter 3

Grief as a Path to Understanding

———•———

Grief is an instinctive reaction to loss, one that can lead you toward deeper insight and personal evolution. In this section, you are invited to look at how Buddhist wisdom—especially the Four Noble Truths—can guide you through the grieving process.

- By viewing grief through the Four Noble Truths, you will come to see it as a form of suffering to be understood rather than resisted.

- Acknowledging impermanence helps you release attachment and ease your aversions.

- In this way, Buddhist teachings offer a roadmap for transforming grief into an opportunity for growth.

GRIEF AND THE FOUR NOBLE TRUTHS

"Life is suffering."

That is what I heard without giving it much thought. OK, without giving it any thought. I quickly rejected the notion that *I* was suffering. I had a happy life. I didn't have a depressed or unhappy bone in my body. A talk about suffering must be for someone else. All I needed was to get back to meditating.

Later, a different teacher said that *dukkha*, which can be translated as suffering, might also be translated as dissatisfaction or dis-ease. We strive for better jobs, fancier cars, or larger homes. We cling to what we have. We try to avoid what we view as unpleasant. We do not want to be sick or experience any difficulties. This is attachment, and it creates *dukkha*. Ah, now that made sense. Like most people, I spent time and energy in my life wanting to move to "the next level" and avoid discomfort. It made sense. My time could be spent in more positive ways.

Yet another teacher offered a helpful story. His mother had a set of costly China. It was beautiful. She kept the dishes in a unique cabinet. She would warn anyone who came within three feet of the China cabinet to watch out. She did not want anyone to bump into the cabinet lest the China fall and break. She used the China once a year for Thanksgiving. She was a nervous wreck the entire time. She told everyone to be careful. Nobody was allowed to hand out the plates or to wash the dishes. Only she could put the dishes back in the China cabinet. The entire time the dishes were out of the cabinet, she was in pure misery. The teacher hated those dishes and how it made his mother a prisoner and made their Thanksgiving so stressful. As he grew older, he began to suggest that they use something else. His mother would have none of that. She insisted that this was the Thanksgiving China. And so it went until one day, his brother's fiancée accidentally knocked her plate off the table.

The entire family watched in horror as the plate fell to the floor, where it broke into several pieces. All at once, everyone turned and looked at his mother and waited. Amazingly, she laughed. And when she finished laughing, she said, "For all of these years I have lived in fear of the China breaking. Now it finally has , and I am finally free!"

Impermanence set her free. She had spent years taking care of those dishes and worrying that they would break yet knowing that eventually they would. That beautiful expensive China brought her no joy. We don't have to spend years clinging to what we deem desirable and pushing away what is undesirable. There is no reason to worry. We need to understand that no matter what we do, one day the China *will* break.

One day *we* will break. Our loved ones *will* die.

You cannot fully embrace impermanence without embracing death. Everything that arises ceases. The way to embrace death is not to ignore it or to deny it; it is to make it a part of your life.

Most of us will encounter a loved one's death before we can fully gain acceptance of death. Quite possibly, it is the death of a loved one that will help you lose *your* fear of death.

When you find yourself experiencing grief, go back to the basics. Revisit the Four Noble Truths. Now, you can use these truths to contemplate your suffering:

1. There is stress and suffering or *dukkha*. Another way to think of this is that in life, we have much dissatisfaction.

In grief, I am experiencing sadness and suffering. This is dissatisfaction. I don't want to feel this way, but here I am. This is what I feel.

2. We experience this dissatisfaction because we become attached to either wanting good things to stay the same or for difficult things to stop being difficult.

In grief, I feel sad. I miss my partner. I did not want him to suffer, but I also did not want him to die. And now, I am alone. I don't want to do this. He would be the one to help me feel better. But he is gone. I wish that were not true. I wish that our lives together could have continued.

3. There is a way out of this dissatisfaction.

In grief, this is hard, but it will not always be this way. It is not going to change overnight, but it will change. And I have the Buddha, the Dhamma, and the Sangha. I have what I need to walk through this suffering.

4. The way out of this dissatisfaction is to live your life per the Noble Eightfold Path.

In grief, right view is my first step on the path. It is right view that allows me to see my suffering for what it is. It helps me to understand that I had an attachment to my loved one. Right view also reminds me that to be sad or to miss my loved one does not make me a bad Buddhist. Now, I can begin to use right intention to help me treat myself with loving-kindness and compassion.

And when I meditate, right mindfulness and right concentration will help me gain even more insight into suffering and attachment and grief. When you are dealing with grief, the Four Noble Truths can become your go-to guide.

You can use contemplations like these or, better yet, develop your own. Find what really speaks to what you are feeling. Developing an understanding of suffering and impermanence will give you strength on your grief journey. Perhaps these fundamental truths are not so basic after all?

ARE MORE PEOPLE THE ANSWER?

If everyone around you is going to die, how can you protect yourself from being without your loved ones? If you assume that your death is still years away, how do you make sure that, when it's your funeral, there will be mourners?

As my parents aged and I wondered and worried about what might happen to them, I began to tell my friends that I wanted to surround them with bubble wrap. And after my father died and my mother started driving again, I wanted to surround her and her car with bubble wrap. And one day, while listening to my mother and her friends talking about their concerns for their children and grandchildren, I realized that they, too, probably wanted guarantees that nothing would happen to their loved ones.

We know there are no guarantees. If I had successfully wrapped anyone in bubble wrap, it would have been suffocating. I would be causing the loss. All of this clinging to our loved ones and loss aversion is difficult. In this passage from the *Visākhā Sutta* (Udana 8.8), we encounter a common reaction to the loss of family.

"I have heard that on one occasion the Blessed One was staying near Sāvatthī at the Eastern Monastery, the palace of Migāra's mother. And on that occasion, a dear and beloved grandson of Visākhā, Migāra's mother, had died. So Visākhā, Migāra's mother—her clothes wet, her *hair wet—went to the Blessed One in the middle of the day, on arrival, having bowed down to him, sat to one side. As she was sitting there the Blessed One said to her: "Why have you come here, Visākhā—your clothes wet, your hair wet—in the middle of the day?"*

When this was said, she said to the Blessed One, "My dear and beloved grandson has died. This is why I have come here—my clothes wet, my hair wet—in the middle of the day."

The Buddha does not offer to bring her grandson back to life. He suggests to her that perhaps she would like to have a larger supply of family. Now, there is an interesting solution. If I had an entire city's worth of friends and family, wouldn't I always have someone? The Buddha specifically names Sāvatthī. During his time, Sāvatthī was a large trade center. Possibly the sixth-largest city in India.

"Visākhā, would you like to have as many children & grandchildren as there are people in Sāvatthī?"

"Yes, lord, I would like to have as many children & grandchildren as there are people in Sāvatthī."

Visākhā thinks that a large family, a family with as many people as those who live in Sāvatthī, is an excellent idea. Maybe it is inconceivable to her to think that death could come for so many people. If she has more people, then when one dies, she still has another. She has lost one grandson; she must be aware of the fact that she can lose more. A bigger collection of children and grandchildren might be a good idea. But the Buddha is not going to give her a family the size of a large city. He is going to give her an understanding of death and of attachment. He is going to help her understand what her wish for such a large family means. He asks her about the death rate in Sāvatthī.

"But how many people in Sāvatthī die in the course of a day?"

"Sometimes ten people die in Sāvatthī in the course of a day, sometimes nine... eight... seven... six... five... four... three... two... Sometimes one person dies in Sāvatthī in the course of a day. Sāvatthī is never free from people dying."

"So, what do you think, Visākhā? Would you ever be free of wet clothes & wet hair?"

"No, lord. Enough of my having so many children & grandchildren."

And there it is. Not only will a family the size of a city not solve the problem. In some ways, it is going to make Visākhā's life much more difficult. She will always be losing someone. This is not a commentary on family planning. It is not meant to tell you to shy away from others. Do not go out and end your loving relationships. If you do, you are still going to experience suffering. By cutting someone off by ending the relationship, you will still experience grief, and you will miss out on enjoying your relationship while you are both alive. What then is the advice for Visākhā, and for us?

- You don't need more people; you need less clinging and aversion. You need more comfort with impermanence.

- Make friends, have good positive relationships. Make sure that you seek to have *kalyāṇa-mittatā* or admirable friendships. These are relationships you make for the right reason—quality, not quantity.

- Don't think that you or your family and friends will be spared. Death comes for all of us.

- Seek to love without attachment.

- Remember that you are not the only one who goes through suffering.

Visākhā was looking for a way to escape the pain that came from losing her grandson. She was trying to find a solution to circumvent death and grief. She went to the Buddha for help. And he did help. He gave her an awareness that as long as she was alive, she would experience the death of others. Every day, there is death. It is not something to be free from, It is something to learn to accept as a normal part of life.

ON RECEIVING THE GIFTS OF IMPERMANENCE, CLINGING, AND AVERSION

During a recent discussion, I referred to impermanence as a gift. To paraphrase, I said that impermanence was the gift that you received that you did not want. You aren't sure that it is a good or useful gift, but then you find yourself using it all the time. It's not extravagant or glamorous, but it is reliable. When you use it regularly and correctly, you will benefit immensely.

Impermanence by itself is incomplete. It is like receiving a toy or other gadget without the batteries. What is missing? Clinging and aversion. Now, I am picturing your face. There you are, opening up the first box or gift bag, and, to your confusion, out comes *impermanence*.

"What am I supposed to do with this?" you exclaim. But there is still another gift to be unwrapped. And so, with optimism, you open it up. Now you can hardly contain your confusion as out comes *attachment*—in two forms, *clinging* and *aversion*.

Congratulations! You have been given a full set of . . . a full set of . . . wait, is there even an instruction booklet or a user guide or something?

Yes, there are instructions. To use these gifts for your full benefit, you need to proceed with awareness. Luckily, you have the Four Noble Truths and the Noble Eightfold Path. The Four Noble Truths remind you that there is dissatisfaction. And that you control your level of stress or dissatisfaction through clinging and aversion. This is not a statement of blame; this is simply an observation of what it means to be human. When you can accept this truth, you will find it easier to navigate impermanence. As you follow the Noble Eightfold Path, you will develop your own deeper understanding of dissatisfaction and how you can ease your stress or suffering.

Whatever stress, in arising, arose for me in the past, all of it had desire as its root, had desire as its cause — for desire is the cause of stress. And whatever stress, in arising, will arise for me in the future, all of it will have desire as the root, will have desire as its cause — for desire is the cause of stress.(SN 42.11)

This is the observation of Gandhabhaka, the headman. He reaches this understanding after the Buddha walks him through some of the finer points of impermanence and attachment, and stress. The primary message in this teaching is about attachment. And this attachment becomes clear when Gandhabhaka is faced with the impermanence of others.

The Blessed One said: "Now what do you think, headman: Are there any people in Uruvelakappa who, if they were murdered or imprisoned or fined or censured, would cause sorrow, lamentation, pain, distress, or despair to arise in you?"

"Yes, lord, there are people in Uruvelakappa who, if they were murdered or imprisoned or fined or censured, would cause sorrow, lamentation, pain, distress, or despair to arise in me."

"And are there any people in Uruvelakappa who, if they were murdered or imprisoned or fined or censured, would cause no sorrow, lamentation, pain, distress, or despair to arise in you?"

"Yes, lord, there are people in Uruvelakappa who, if they were murdered or imprisoned or fined or censured, would cause no sorrow, lamentation, pain, distress, or despair to arise in me."(SN 42.11)

Every instance of the death or misfortune of others does not hold the same level of stress for Gandhabhaka. This teaching does not give us any reason to believe that he actively wishes for the death or misfortune of anyone. Just that there are some people whose demise would be more painful for him. With the arising of compassion and equanimity, his experience would be different. But this is not the purpose of the teaching. On this occasion, Gandhabhaka has specifically asked the Buddha to teach him the origin and ending of stress. And to make sure that Gandhabhaka is understanding the lesson, the Buddha continues:

"Now what is the cause, what is the reason, why the murder, imprisonment, fining, or censure of some of the people in Uruvelakappa would cause you sorrow, lamentation, pain, distress, or despair, whereas the murder imprisonment, fining, or censure of others would cause you no sorrow, lamentation, pain, distress, or despair?"

"Those people in Uruvelakappa whose murder, imprisonment, fining, or censure would cause me sorrow, lamentation, pain, distress, or despair are those for whom I feel desire & passion. Those people in Uruvelakappa whose murder, imprisonment, fining, or censure would cause me no

sorrow, lamentation, pain, distress, or despair are those for whom I feel no desire or passion." (SN 42.11)

The difference is the depth of Gandhabhaka's feelings. To make this even clearer, the Buddha asks how Gandhabhaka would feel if his son were to experience death or misfortune. The Buddha also asks how Gandhabhaka would feel if his wife experienced death or misfortune. And in both cases, Gandhabhaka acknowledges that he would be devastated.

In contemplating his loved ones experiencing misfortune or in considering their deaths, Gandhabhaka gains an understanding of the cause of stress. And that understanding is gleaned from the skillful teachings he received. Teachings that used *impermanence* and *clinging*, and *aversion*.

LET CLINGING
BE YOUR TEACHER

In grief, there is *dukkha*. The most obvious reason for this is that we want whatever it is that we have lost to come back to us, or we wish never to have experienced the loss at all, or we do not want to feel all of the complex emotions that, for many of us, are part of grieving. We become attached to either wanting good things to stay the same or for difficult things to stop being difficult: I want this, and I do not want that.

There it is, clinging and aversion. If this is not true for you, then now is a great time to stop reading. Or perhaps continue and gain an understanding of what other people around you are experiencing every day.

When someone you love dies, the most apparent form of attachment is your attachment to your relationship. Now your mother, father, partner, or friend has gone. He or she is not coming down the hall to have breakfast with you. You are not going on vacation together. He or she will not make you dinner, do the dishes, or take out the trash. You will have times when you forget this, and you will look for him or her when you come into the room. Or you will try to send a text. Or you will think, "Oh, I need to tell Mom about . . ." And then you will remember, "Oh, that's right. Mom is dead." And it will hurt. It will hurt less as you remind yourself about clinging and attachment and impermanence. It will hurt less when you accept the situation for what it is and learn how to live your life as it is now.

There are other forms of clinging and aversion that might be part of your journey. Sometimes they are so subtle that you do not recognize them, while other times, it just smacks you in the face. What are some of these forms?

Things

A few days after my father died, my mother went to his closet and pulled out his clothing. She was distraught and could not stand to look at his things. At the time, I was shocked. On some level, I recognized that she was having an emotional reaction to his death, and seeing his clothing was triggering. A few weeks later, as she was walking down the hallway, she had a similar episode. She insisted that his computer desk needed to be taken apart and moved into the garage right away. Fortunately, I was able to comply. She had an aversion to seeing the things he used daily because he was no longer here, using those things. And seeing his jacket in the closet or his empty desk was breaking her heart.

My aunt kept her husband's clothing precisely as it was for over a year. His closet was ready and waiting for his return. Nobody was allowed to touch anything. In this state, her new husband moved in and found a way to make room for his things.

You might find yourself in one of the above scenarios. Or you might find yourself letting things go in phases. I know I have felt this happen to me.

There were some items that I released right away. As I write this, I can visualize some of the things I still have.

There is a lesson in what you keep and what you release. What do you cling to and why? What do you get rid of and why? I had no problem selling my husband's gold watch. I never liked that watch. The circumstances under which he received the watch were somewhat sketchy. He knew that, but he loved the look of it. Now, years later, I still have his favorite old tank top. I am never going to wear it. I do not take it out and look at it. But I can tell you exactly where it is.

Roles

In the selfing that you do, and in your clinging to the ego, you create roles for yourself. Your version and vision of who you are. The part that you have selected for yourself may or may not support you. How do you know? By watching yourself. Sit with your beliefs about who you are and how your behaviors bring you ease or bring discomfort. If, during this time, you cling to your role as the strong one, or the emotional one, or the drama queen, or the energy vampire, you are binding yourself to suffer from a fetter. The more that you hang on to your role, the more you think, "I am strong, I should be able to handle this," or "I should be recovering faster," or "I should not feel sad anymore." All of these thoughts are just adding to your suffering.

Emotions

To live with grief is to live with an ever-changing cornucopia of emotions. Happy, sad, fearful, hopeful, and so much more. Not only is each day different, but sometimes each moment is too. There is good news. Whatever you are feeling is OK. You are not your feelings, and your feelings will change. Feel the difficult emotions. Sit with them. Watch them rise, notice how and where you feel them, and watch them cease.

You are not required to hang onto any of it. You do not have to tell people that everything is great when it is not great. You also do not have to tell everyone that things are terrible if they are not terrible. There is no required time limit on any of your emotions. If you find yourself pushing away the problematic emotions, pay attention to your aversion. What is behind not wanting to recognize your pain?

Surroundings

After my husband died, I remember people just assuming that I would move. And at first, I assumed that I would move too. It was not because I wanted to move, but because, for a brief time, I thought I should move. Now, I see this as one of how different types of clinging and aversion come together. My role as a partner had changed. People around me thought I should not be alone in this space. Some of those people had their aversion to having to see me in a place that used to belong to us. When sitting with it and investigating what came up for me, I realized that I was perfectly happy staying in my current space. I was not walking around the house creating memorials or seeing my dead husband in every corner. I was happy and secure. Others hate staying behind in a space that they shared with a loved one. Whether you stay or go, pay attention to your clinging and aversion. The truth is that whatever decision you make might be triggered by your attachment. And the first step toward working with it is recognition.

There are so many lessons for you in what you hang on to and what you push away. These are not simply lessons about our relationship with our loved ones. They are lessons about our relationship with ourselves and with life itself. The *Alagaddupama Sutta* is a teaching that can be useful in showing us how to be skillful with our attachments.

"*Suppose a man were traveling along a path. He would see a great expanse of water, with the near shore dubious and risky, the further shore secure and free from risk, but with neither a ferryboat nor a bridge going from this shore to the other. The thought would occur to him, 'Here is this great expanse of water, with the near shore dubious and risky, the further shore secure and free from risk, but with neither a ferryboat nor a bridge going from this shore to the other. What if I were to gather grass, twigs, branches, and leaves and, having bound them together to make a raft, were to cross over to safety on the other shore in dependence on the raft, making an effort with my hands and feet?' Then the man, having gathered grass, twigs, branches, and leaves, having bound them together to make a raft, would cross over to safety on the other shore in dependence on the raft, making an effort with his hands and feet. Having crossed over to the further shore, he might think, 'How useful this raft has been to me! For it was in dependence on this raft that, making an effort with my hands and feet, I have crossed over to safety on the further shore. Why don't I, having hoisted it on my head or carrying it on my back, go wherever I like?' What*

do you think, monks: Would the man, in doing that, be doing what should be done with the raft?'
"'No, lord.'

"And what should the man do in order to be doing what should be done with the raft? There is the case where the man, having crossed over, would think, 'How useful this raft has been to me! For it was in dependence on this raft that, making an effort with my hands and feet, I have crossed over to safety on the further shore. Why don't I, having dragged it on dry land or sinking it in the water, go wherever I like?' In doing this, he would be doing what should be done with the raft." (MN 22)

There will be things, emotions, surroundings, and more that will be part of your grief journey. Some of these you will want to gather up and use to create your raft. And that raft will be an essential part of your trip. Conversely, the day will also come when you realize that those things, emotions, or surroundings slow you down. It is time to let go of your raft.

Chapter 4

The Wisdom of Impermanence

———•———

Have you ever noticed how everything around you is in flux? In Buddhism, impermanence teaches you that change is the only true constant. By welcoming this ever-shifting nature of life, you open yourself up to freedom and inner calm.

Here are some gentle reminders to carry with you:

- Embrace impermanence as a doorway to wisdom. When you see change not as a threat but as a natural flow, your heart grows lighter.

- Cultivate equanimity to navigate life's peaks and valleys. With balanced acceptance, you can celebrate joys without clinging and meet challenges without fear.

- Let the truth of impermanence free you from attachment. Releasing what no longer serves you brings presence—and in presence, your life will unfold. It will be a different life, you will be a different person, but you will live!

DEATH AND EQUANIMITY

Name Two Things that Belong Together?

And the answer is: *death and equanimity.*

Knock Knock! (A *haiku*)

Oh, it's you again.
Really? No place else to be?
OK, death—come in.

I remember driving to pick up a refill of Dad's morphine prescription. He was definitely in his final stages with lung cancer. All around me in the drug store were people just going about their business. Teenage girls looking at the makeup, a woman buying greeting cards, and a father buying ice cream for his children. I recall thinking, Dad used to buy me ice cream, too. And now he never will again. It was hard to understand how all of these people could just be going about their business.

When Mom and my husband Ed died, I recall having a similar reaction. I would see people running their errands, buying groceries, filling up their gas tanks. Didn't they know that I was utterly torn up? Eventually, I began to see the routines of others as reassuring. Watching people navigate the everyday business of life gave me hope. Others were well and happy. And I would be, too. It was good to be surrounded by people who did not seem to be impacted by death. Of course, I had no idea how many of them were watching the rest of us and thinking, "How can they just be going about their business, don't they know my loved one has died?"

Equanimity helped me to watch all of these experiences, and to smile at the father buying his daughter ice cream, and to wish *mettā* to the woman at the pump across from mine at the gas station. I did not know what other experiences life had brought them. I did know that at some point, they would experience sadness. And if today I saw them experiencing joy, then I was happy for their joy.

Equanimity helped me to accept the importance of living the life that I had been given and to realize that, already having experienced difficulty, was no guarantee that there would not be more.

My friends would say things like, "Well, you are done now. You have already had some difficult experiences. There is no way that life [or God, if that was their belief system], would send you anything else to deal with. That just would not be fair."

But it is not about fairness or about what you have had to deal with. Many people have dealt with situations that are much more difficult. People have lost their entire families in one tragic moment.

Your karma will send you what it sends you. That does not mean that your life is fatefully predetermined. It means that based on your past and current actions, your karma will take root. And you will live the fruits of your karma. Equanimity brings you a balanced perspective. It helps you to set your priorities. You understand that it makes no sense to spend your energy on your past actions. Own these actions and the karma that stems from them. Do your best with what comes your way. Do not use your energy wishing that your loved ones would not die. Use your actions skillfully to help yourself and to help others.

I cannot go back in time and change anything about my current or past lives. Time travel storylines, while fun, are inherently flawed. You are only supposed to change one thing, but if you change other things the universe is damned forever. You are never supposed to meet yourself in another dimension, or the universe is damned forever. Forget about all that. It is much easier to just work on your life as you live it right now.

Not knowing what will come but knowing that whatever happens is part of your karma is less stressful than worrying about what is coming. Grief is something to learn from and not simply to be endured. It is not a series of mile markers on a racetrack. There is no need to rush through any part of your life; it is all as it is meant to be. You need to keep practicing.

Expectations for a life completely without *dukkha* are unreasonable. It is our *views* that make a situation either easy or difficult, to be avoided or to be embraced. Equanimity and compassion, and loving-kindness help us to see our role in our suffering.

Equanimity means that we accept death. It is one of the many events that make up our lives. In one moment, you might be with a friend who has just lost her husband, and in the next moment, you receive a text that your other friend is newly engaged. On the same day, you might learn that a former co-worker has died, and then you receive a text about someone else's new baby.

All of these moments are important and are meant to be experienced with equanimity. This does not mean without feeling. It means to direct your energy and emotions in the best possible way. Be happy for your newly engaged friend. Don't be manic about it. Be sad at the loss of your co-worker. Understand the truth—that you cannot feel everything for everybody. You cannot prevent others from having difficulties, and you are rarely the cause of their gains. YOU are not karma.

I won't promise you that death will become easy for you. That death is no big deal, and that you will not be sad when someone dies, or that you will not cry. I won't tell you that because it is not true. What I will say is that your relationship with death can become much more balanced. Equanimity will help you see that death has its place in the overall landscape of your life.

THE PROMISE
OF IMPERMANENCE

Mary Carol woke up with an upset stomach. This did not fit with her plans for the day. She was going to have brunch with some friends. She took some antacids and continued getting ready. Eventually, her stomach would settle down. When it was time to leave, not only had her stomach not settled down, but she felt worse. The antacids had done nothing, and now she felt slightly nauseous. Mentally, she changed her goals for the outing, going from enjoying food and friends to enjoying friends. She got into her car and began her drive.

About 20 minutes into her 40-minute drive, Mary Carol realized that she was really feeling ill. And the mere idea of food made her stomach turn flip-flops. She wondered if anyone would notice if she did not order anything more than a sparkling water or perhaps a 7-Up? She began to feel confident that if she ate anything, it would come right back up. And with that thought, she exited the freeway, pulled over, and called to advise the brunch coordinator that she was not going to make it. Then she began her commute back home. She made it through the door just in time to become ill. She took off her festive brunch outfit and crawled under the blankets. Her stomach pain increased. She had a fever, and eventually her system emptied itself of all its contents.

After she made the decision to return home and had climbed into bed, Mary Carol realized that what she was going to do that day was be sick.

That was how it was going to be, and actually, all she needed to do was to be with her illness. Her activity for the day was to be sick. And as her fever rose and the pain intensified, she practiced some deep meditative breathing. She worked on simply being with the discomfort, with an awareness that at some point it would stop. Food poisoning or a virus (whichever it was) was impermanent. That knowledge helped her. You can say that she was clinging to the idea that all the discomfort would subside.

After a few hours, Mary Carol woke up. She felt sore and a little bit warm, but the majority of the illness seemed to have passed. In this instance, her assumption that impermanence meant the discomfort would go away was correct. At any point during her illness, her situation might have changed in a way that she would have perceived as much more difficult—perhaps the removal of her appendix, or some other surgery, or a lasting malady. Impermanence is not a promise of improvement.

More than one medieval Persian Sufi poet referenced the phrase, "And this, too, shall pass away." In its original usage, the phrase was an elegant way of observing that both sorrows and joys would come and go. A description of the human condition, in good times and in bad. Today, a variation of this sentiment exists in multiple cultures. Mary Carol had heard her friends say it to one another during difficult times. They used it as a way to remind each other that hard times would give way to better times. Perhaps Mary Carol had even uttered this to herself as she curled up with her stomach pain. This is not the promise of impermanence.

Impermanence is not a reassurance that things will get better. It is not a simple reminder that change will come. Impermanence reminds us that form and consciousness will disintegrate. We come apart. Consider these passages from the *Mahā Parinibbāna Sutta* (DN 16). In the first, the Buddha is reminding his disciples that even he will fall.

"Has it not already been repeatedly said by me that there is separation, division, and parting from all that is dear and beloved? How could it be that what is born, comes to being, formed, and is liable to fall, should not fall? That is not possible."

And when the Buddha had passed away, Sakka, the chief of the deities, uttered the following:

Impermanent are all component things,
They arise and cease, that is their nature:
They come into being and pass away,
Release from them is bliss supreme.

Our disintegration is not always obvious. We live in such a way that we see continuity. We go to sleep, we wake up, and most days everything seems to be the same. But the reality is inconstancy. Little by little, we are changing. One of my teachers likes to remind us of this by suggesting that we look at our photos from a few years ago. For most of us, looking at those photos and then looking in the mirror is all we need to see the signs of our inconstancy.

It's not wrong that Mary Carol believed her stomach pain would get better. Most of the time, she is going to be right. Food poisoning or a virus will go away. In most cases, she will experience a change for the better. And being with her suffering, noticing the feeling of discomfort, and breathing through it, is a good practice. It is also to her benefit to remember that impermanence is not a promise that all difficulties pave the way for easier times. It is her practice that will help her find a way to embrace impermanence with more ease.

IMPERMANENCE IS IN SIGHT

"That's the way it is, Ananda. When young, one is subject to aging; when healthy, subject to illness; when alive, subject to death. The complexion is no longer so clear & bright; the limbs are flabby & wrinkled; the back, bent forward; there's a discernible change in the faculties — the faculty of the eye, the faculty of the ear, the faculty of the nose, the faculty of the tongue, the faculty of the body." (SN 48.41)

Impermanence was coming for my eyes. I knew this because it had been only two years since my eye doctor told me I needed a new prescription for my driving glasses. And now, when I wore those glasses, they seemed off. The vision change was small yet noticeable. Yet I felt confident that I was not a risk to other drivers.

A recent visit to the DMV (Department of Motor Vehicles) confirmed my suspicions. While going through the steps of renewing my driver's license, I put on my glasses and took the vision test. After I finished calling out the numbers and letters to the man administering the exam, he looked at me and, with a face devoid of expression, said, "You missed one." Then he told me to continue to the next step, which was to take an updated photo. I correctly assumed that missing one was not a huge deal, and so I had passed the test. The DMV trusted me to drive with my glasses on.

Two weeks later, with thoughts of these events in mind, I drove to my yearly check-up with my eye doctor. I was mentally prepared for the fact that my vision had declined further and that I would need new lenses. I packed an older backup pair to reuse my current frames. And as she led me through reading the various eye charts, the doctor and I caught up on what had transpired in our lives over the past year. As the tests ended, she wrote some notes in my chart, looked up, and said, "Your distance vision has changed."

Here it was, the moment that I knew had been coming. She went on: "You no longer need your driving glasses." It must have been worse than I thought. What comes after glasses? A headset with securely attached goggles? Sensing my confusion, she explained that my vision had gotten better. She used a human eye diagram to teach me how, sometimes, our vision can improve. It took me a moment to process this information. She told me, "You can keep wearing your glasses if you like, they're not hurting you, but now they're also not helping you."

I drove away with my glasses on because I had 25 years of attachment to wearing them. And the same number of years making the same stupid joke: "Well, the DMV wants me to see things *before* I run into them."

In some Native American stories, the coyote is known as a trickster. He ignores the rules and can be a bit of a con artist. Reports of his antics serve as reminders to live honestly and follow societal norms. When I learn that my eyesight has improved, I am tempted to think that impermanence is a trickster, too. But impermanence did not trick me. I did that all by myself. I felt the change, worked with some resistance around the difference, and then moved forward confidently, knowing what was coming.

But with true impermanence or *anicca* (Pāli), we do not know for sure what is coming. We learn to expect inconstancy. Yes, logically, as I grow older, there will be changes that will restrict my vision or mobility. Are those negative changes? My doctor described this as an improvement in my eyesight. That sounds good. Yet, if I cling to the view that this is good, what happens the next time my eyesight changes? What if next year my doctor says to me, "Time to put those glasses back on"?

In the time between when I realized that my eyesight had improved and I began to drive home, there was a part of me that wanted to be self-congratulatory. Like all those false advertisements and unrealistic expectations, I was getting older and better. Somewhere, another part of me remembered *upekkha* or equanimity. Best to take all of this in stride; to accept this news in a balanced and even-minded manner. It would be easier to make more out of this than it is. To grab on to this change in my vision and to become attached. Perhaps to expect even more. To forget that none of this is me, nor does it belong to me. But that is the way to *dukkha*.

IT'S THE LITTLE THINGS

"What do you mean by death with a lower-case 'd'?"

"How does impermanence help us face the bigger challenges in life?"

Upon the launch of Season 2 of the Death Dhamma podcast, these two questions came to me from two different groups. The answer was that in Season 2, we do not explicitly discuss the death of a loved sentient being. Instead, we discuss the other types of death we experience; death with a lower-case "d." In the course of your lifetime, you will experience loss. Sometimes the loss might be minuscule: you went to the store for mint chocolate chip ice cream, and it was sold out. You had to select something else. And in that moment, you experienced the loss of your ability to fulfill your craving for mint chocolate chip ice cream. Other losses feel much more significant: the end of a relationship, or your job is eliminated, or your car is totaled in an accident.

These are the types of losses that can be called death with a lower-case "d." On any given day, you have things that you believe went well, meaning you believe that you got what you wanted, and you have things that did not go according to your plan. This leads us to consider how impermanence can help us face the bigger challenges in life.

It is how you handle these various losses that prepare you for the bigger challenges you will face. I described the inability to buy your favorite flavor of ice cream as a minuscule loss. What do you think? How do you react when you cannot have your mint chocolate chip? Do you accept it, select another flavor, and move on? Or do you take it as a personal affront, perhaps inspiring a rant along the lines of, "They know this is a popular flavor, why can't they keep it in stock? Who does the ordering? I should complain. I just wanted this one small thing; can't I even have that? Don't I deserve my favorite ice cream at the end of a hard day?" While some very entitled people do rise to the occasion during times of loss, for many of us, how we handle these lesser challenges can be an indicator of our ability to deal with death with a capital "D"—when a sentient being we love dies and when we face our mortality.

Your Buddhist practice gives you the tools you need to build your resilience. The Four Noble Truths remind you that there is dissatisfaction. And you control your level of dissatisfaction through clinging and aversion. This is not a statement of blame. This is an observation of what it means to be human. When you can accept this truth, you will find it easier to navigate impermanence.

Start small. You do not have to immediately go right to "I am going to die!" You can benefit from truly reflecting on the truth that there is suffering and on the source of that suffering: wanting things, people, and outcomes, and also from not wanting other things, or people, or outcomes. You want your favorite ice cream; you do not want to have to make another choice.

You know that things are always changing. And the more we hang on to our perceptions of how things must be, the more difficult our lives become. If you did experience strong negative emotions over the ice cream, what did that do to your day? Your blood pressure went up, you felt anger, you experienced tension in your body. You had hard feelings toward the store or the employees. And this disrupted other events and probably your interactions with others. And these reactions did not magically make your ice cream appear. Next time, you can try going to the store with an open mind. You are going to buy your favorite ice cream. If that flavor is not available, you have a second and possibly a third choice. And, if there is no ice cream, you have another choice, or you are not attached to having ice cream at all.

When our plans fall apart, we are presented with an opportunity to embrace impermanence. Those broken plans are a representation of death. Something you relied upon went away. An assumption becomes invalid, a cherished thing breaks, a relationship ends. Pay attention to your emotions as you watch your plans die. Pay attention to your emotions as you begin to watch your plans die, with acceptance. As you begin to become comfortable with how uncertainty is always a part of your daily life. You can begin to project beyond your daily plans.

The plans you have made for your week, your month, your year, all of this is built on a perception of control and an illusion of certainty. Yet plans help us to navigate our lives. Keep making plans and, as you do so, acknowledge that there will be impermanence. Some of your plans, or elements of your plans will die. And when this happens, call it death. Remind yourself that this is a type of death. Now you are living with death.

This is how death with a lower-case "d" and impermanence work to help you become more resilient. Being resilient does not mean never feeling disappointment or anger or sadness, it means feeling these emotions and not allowing them to run your life.

Dancing Around Death: Meeting Denial with Courage and Compassion

Many of us in the West have been taught to avoid the subject of death. It is something we hide away from; we discuss death softly, in hushed tones, if we discuss it at all. Sometimes we use language that makes it seem as if the deceased has done something wrong. We seek to uncover *why* someone has died and to find a way to make it their fault. We say things like: "After a brave and valiant fight, she lost her battle with cancer." We use this language so often that we might not even think about what we are saying. Would you call your best friend who died from ovarian cancer a loser? Of course not. This kind of phrasing is so embedded in our discussions around death that we do not even realize that what we are saying is that she tried, but she failed. I get it: I used similar words in an obituary once myself. I tried so hard not to, but I did not know what else to say. Now I understand that what I wanted to convey was that someone had died: he had cancer, and he did an awesome job of living his life with cancer until it was his time to die. To die is not a failure. It is a natural and inevitable part of our human experience.

Death denial is a coping mechanism deeply ingrained in the human psyche. A psychological defense mechanism that allows us to avoid confronting the inevitability of death, it also prevents us from developing a deep bond with impermanence, blocking our spiritual growth, and preventing us from moving toward a release from suffering.

Engaging in death denial offers a sense of comfort and protection from the anxiety and fear of the unknown aspects of death. It allows us to maintain a semblance of normalcy in our lives. Death denial provides a false sense of protection from the difficult emotions that surface when we think about our own death or the death of our loved ones. I say false sense of protection because the real protection comes from understanding the Dhamma.

Denying the inevitability of death can hinder our ability to live authentically and to fully embrace life in all its complexities. By avoiding discussions about death, we fail to address important end-of-life wishes and plans with our loved ones. Discussing death does not have to be gloomy or depressing. By engaging in conversations about death and dying, we can cultivate a deeper appreciation for life, strengthen our relationships, and gain a newfound perspective on what truly matters. Embracing the dance of life means acknowledging the reality of death with grace and compassion.

Emotional avoidance of death can lead us to anxiety, depression, or unresolved grief. When we develop the ability to have open conversations about mortality, we create deeper connections with our loved ones. And when we acknowledge our own fears, we are stepping toward a more peaceful existence.

Openness to thoughts and discussions about death support us in our Buddhist practice. By embracing the reality of death with courage and compassion, we can transform our fear of death into a source of wisdom and enlightenment. Courage supports us as we move forward to confront difficult topics, and compassion supports us when we turn away, or take a step or two back from difficult topics. We start with ourselves, with our aversion to death, and then we can work with others. In this way, we have a solid foundation on which we can rely. Truthfully, we usually find ourselves dealing with our thoughts and emotions about death while interacting with others. For example, when a beloved family member is dying, other family members will have different responses and different degrees of preparedness. Rarely is there a perfect scenario in which you have had the opportunity to be completely in a place of equanimity around the death of a parent, sibling, or partner.

Have the courage to do what is needed to take of yourself and to acknowledge the difficult thoughts and emotions that are surfacing. Perhaps you are not as prepared for this death as you would like. Have the compassion to accept yourself as you are. Bravely continue on, face your fears, and recognize denial when it arises. Know that others around you are in a different place. Perhaps, there is someone who appears to be handling this more serenely. If this is true, can you spend more time with that person and learn about the source of their strength? Some may be falling apart, while others are in deep denial, not even willing to accept that death is imminent. You might find the behaviors of others too much to process. This, too, is a call for courage and compassion. You might need to separate yourself, or you might draw on your reserves to be with others in a way that does not leave you in shambles. Be aware of the limits of your endurance. Use compassion toward others to help you accept where they are with death denial and use compassion toward yourself when you need to step away. Don't forget to support yourself with time for contemplation—even if that is a short walking meditation around the hospital floor or a micro-meditation in your parked car.

Compassion toward ourselves and others in the face of death denial helps us to create a nonjudgmental environment. From this place of acceptance, we can approach the topic of death with patience and understanding. It might take many attempts to get the conversation started. Some people are never going to join you in this space. Others will eventually open up and share their fears, concerns, and beliefs. Continuing to revisit an unpopular topic does take courage, and when others join the discussion, they, too, are coming from a place of bravery. Engaging in these conversations can lead to deeper connections with the people around us and help us all feel less isolated.

Through courage and compassion, we can navigate the complexities of death denial and find peace in the knowledge that our time on this Earth is finite.

WE ARE THE
FLOWERS IN THE GARDEN

Once, while I was visiting my mother, she looked out of the window and saw some strangers wandering around in her backyard. She opened the sliding glass door and asked, "Can I help you with something?"

Sheepishly, one of the visitors replied: "We heard about your garden and we just wanted to take a peek."

My mother had a beautiful English garden. It was her pride and joy. I know for a fact that on the morning that she died, she had worked in her garden. Which is exactly what she would have wanted. Sometimes, when I visited, we would walk through the garden together. She would give me a tour; while pulling a weed or two, she would teach me which plants should be near one another, and what to plant to stave off intrusive insects or aggressive vines. She carefully cultivated each section of her garden, paying regular, focused attention to what was or was not working and adjusting as needed. I view her garden and her work as an analogy for our own spiritual practice.

"I don't envision a single thing that, when undeveloped & uncultivated, leads to such great harm as the mind. The mind, when undeveloped & uncultivated leads to great harm."

"I don't envision a single thing that, when developed & cultivated, leads to such great benefit as the mind. The mind, when developed & cultivated, leads to great benefit."

"I don't envision a single thing that, when undeveloped & uncultivated, brings about such suffering & stress as the mind. The mind, when undeveloped & uncultivated, brings about suffering & stress."

"I don't envision a single thing that, when developed & cultivated, brings about such happiness as the mind. The mind, when developed & cultivated, brings about happiness." (AN 1: 27–30)

We are like the flowers in the garden. We require careful cultivation. To grow in our practice, we need to place ourselves in an appropriate environment, surrounded by the right companionship, placing regular, focused attention through learning and meditating , and following the Noble Eightfold Path.

During our garden tours, Mom would often cut back or completely remove a dead or dying plant. On more than one occasion, she said to me: "There is a lot of death in the garden." Her tone was very matter of fact. Her statement came from a place of *this is how it is*.

Mom never let gardening deaths and disappointments get the better of her. She had a very good understanding of the expected lifespans of her plants. She was not completely surprised if a raccoon dug up her bulbs, or if a passing deer bit the head off of a flower, or if a plant seemed to die randomly. Occasionally, she would express annoyance at the raccoons and the deer, and disappointment when a plant did not work out, but she did not dwell on it.

Mom gardened with non-attachment. With a complete understanding of horticultural impermanence, she did not avoid a flower that would bloom quickly and then fade away. She would showcase that flower. Finding a way to surround it with plants that would allow it to have a brief moment of stardom. Then, the surrounding plants would have their turn. And eventually, they too would disappear. Within the context of her garden, Mom understood the truth of aging and death. She knew that once planted, a flower would bloom and then die.

"The aging of beings in the various orders of beings, their old age, brokenness of teeth, grayness of hair, wrinkling of skin, decline of life, weakness of faculties — this is called aging. The passing of beings out of the various orders of beings, their passing away, dissolution, disappearance, dying, completion of time, dissolution of the aggregates, laying down of the body — this is called death. So this aging and this death are what is called aging and death. With the arising of birth there is the arising of aging and death." (MN 9.22)

We are like the flowers in the garden. Once we are planted and begin to grow, we will die. And others around us will die. Take a look at a garden, a park, or a forest. There might be tall and mighty trees that are more than a hundred years old. Then there is a flowering ground cover that shows up in early spring and fades away with the summer heat. There are rose bushes, which last several seasons. And, perhaps, tulips or daffodils that pop up once a year; they have one bloom, and they are done.

Do not let the concept of impermanence discourage you. When the meaning of impermanence is misunderstood, it can push you toward nihilism. Some develop an attitude of "if nothing lasts, why bother?" If my mother had taken this point of view, she would have missed out on all the joy she felt while gardening. Her neighbors would have been denied the opportunity of walking past such beautiful scenery.

Go all in. Instead of avoiding experiences in life, learn the most you can from those experiences. Instead of avoiding relationships with others, be fully in those relationships, without attachment. Learn from the present moment because it will be gone. Don't think, "Why bother? This will not last." Do think: "This opportunity will not be here again. Let me be in this moment and let it be my teacher." Like my mother with her garden, be skillful in how you cultivate your practice and your mind. Be aware of death. And let it encourage you to live.

What arises, ceases. With each passing moment, even the strongest, sturdiest tree becomes closer to death. Today, petunias might be blooming, yet they will wilt under the hot summer Sun. It is not about if we and our loved ones will die, it is when.

Chapter 5

Cultivating Compassion and Resilience

———•———

Self-compassion and emotional resilience are strong allies on your journey. When you greet yourself with kindness and curiosity, you open the door to genuine healing and meaningful growth. Rather than turning away from difficult feelings, learn to meet them with mindful presence, recognizing even your most challenging emotions as teachers. As you draw on timeless Buddhist wisdom, you will discover simple yet profound practices—like gentle awareness of breath and the invitation to observe thoughts without judgment. These are the types of practices that will carry you through life's inevitable emotional storms. In nurturing these qualities, you begin to walk more confidently in the world, carrying a quiet strength born of inner kindness and clear-eyed acceptance.

TO SAY GOODBYE TO SUFFERING, SAY HELLO TO DIFFICULT EMOTIONS

Dealing with the loss of a loved one and the intense emotions that surface while you grieve is easy, said NO ONE EVER! At least, no one I have met. I am not sure how much I would trust someone who would call grief easy to navigate.

In 2021, 12 different Buddhist teachers spoke to me about death and grief, and Buddhism. They came from various Buddhist traditions. Some were monks or nuns, some were lay practitioners, and each had spent various amounts of time on their respective paths. All of them recounted having strong feelings when their loved ones died. And several of them had encountered expectations from others around not feeling or acknowledging emotion. Some people expressed a belief that being Buddhist should have made them immune to dealing with difficult emotions. Or, when faced with sadness or regret, a "good" Buddhist can just cut off those emotions. Just. Cut. Them. Off. As if there is a point in our practice where we have a pair of invisible emotion-cutting scissors. Maybe I am not far enough along to have earned my scissors, but I think that no matter how far on the path I tread, there are no scissors.

Buddhist practice is not about cutting off your feelings. It is about meeting them. When emotions arise, do not try to turn them off. Repeatedly, the discussions I had with others would eventually land on the importance of being *with* your feelings. As human beings, we often resist facing challenging emotions. When it comes to dealing with death, the resistance is strong. One of my 12 teachers told a story of speaking about Buddhism to a delegation from France. As part of the talk, he introduced the topic of death. A reminder that we will all pass. When the conversation was over, one of the representatives approached him and admonished him for being inappropriate. The representative said that "we" do not talk about things like that. This and some other experiences showed him that there is a preference in much of Western society to hide death and shy away from discussing our impermanence.

Another teacher encountered students who thought that Buddhism would help them avoid all of the complicated feelings. That being enlightened means to be like a stone. Perhaps some interpret the point of the teachings, as expressed below, as a war on suffering. Winning that war requires not even allowing difficult emotions to surface.

"And how is liberation its core? Here, the teachings have been taught by me to my disciples for the utterly complete destruction of suffering. Through liberation one experiences those teachings in just the way that I have taught them to my disciples for the utterly complete destruction of suffering. It is in this way that liberation is its core." (AN 4.245)

I can think of one or two individuals in our meditation group who will tell people that they need to cut off their feelings. When you are meditating, and feelings distract you, just cut those feelings off.

This shortest of *suttas* acknowledges feelings:

"Bhikkhus, there are these three feelings. What three? Pleasant feeling, unpleasant feeling, and neither-painful-nor-pleasant feeling." SN 36.30

Fortunately, when someone advises others to cut off their feelings, our lead teacher will gently break in and suggest a different approach, reminding all of us that the answer is *not* to cut off feelings. The answer is to have the feeling. To greet it. To inwardly say, "Oh hello sadness, what will you teach me today?"

To acknowledge and to be with your emotions does not mean that you become those emotions. This is an important distinction, especially for those who come from just cutting off anything that causes discomfort. Just because you notice sadness arising does not mean you have to *become* sad. Just see that, oh, sadness is here. This is in keeping with this passage from the *Satipatthana Sutta*:

"And how does a monk remain focused on feelings in and of themselves? There is the case where a monk, when feeling a painful feeling, discerns, 'I am feeling a painful feeling.' When feeling a pleasant feeling, he discerns, 'I am feeling a pleasant feeling.' When feeling a neither-painful-nor-pleasant feeling, he discerns, 'I am feeling a neither-painful-nor-pleasant feeling.'" (MN 10)

Discerning or noticing the feeling does not require you to go all in with that feeling. Maybe you are not strong enough to become one with your grief. It is to your benefit to be open to it. And to be compassionate of yourself and your experience as you feel it arising. Try observing how you have armored yourself. Have you tried to run away from the idea of losing a loved one? Have you tried to ignore it? You start by noticing the feeling. Do you feel it in your body? How does it feel? You are both the observer and the observed. You are connecting with your grief and how it impacts you. And as you watch it, you will see that as suffering arises, it will also eventually fall. It will come back again, and it will leave too. Using an expression that is less elegant than the *suttas*: the only way out is *through*. No magic scissors are involved.

The acknowledgment of complicated feelings is not the entire path to liberation. The *Satipatthana Sutta* teaches us to focus on the body, mind, and mental qualities in addition to emotions.

The *sutta* concludes:

"'This is the direct path for the purification of beings, for the overcoming of sorrow and lamentation, for the disappearance of pain and distress, for the attainment of the right method, and for the realization of Unbinding—in other words, the four frames of reference.' Thus was it said, and in reference to this was it said." (MN 10)

WHERE THERE IS GRIEF, LET THERE BE COMPASSION

When your grief is fresh and raw, you need compassion. You are your most important source. To be with your grief without being constantly overwhelmed by it requires tremendous self-compassion. When someone you love dies, you are forever changed. At first, the changes you experience can be stressful. You might not sleep, you might sleep all day, you might not eat, you might eat comfort food, you might want to lose yourself in movies or shows, or you might wander around your home feeling fitful and lost, unable to concentrate for more than a moment. You might crave solitude; you might be afraid to be alone. I always remember my aunt saying to me: "Remember, you are not in your right mind." As annoyed as I was by her comment, I also knew that she was correct. And there was very little to do about my state other than to continue to be compassionate toward myself. Each day I was doing my best. Somedays that meant I was fully functional, and other days it was all I could do to get out of bed and wash my face.

Self-compassion is not an excuse to indulge in harmful or unhealthy habits. It is not a reason to ignore your responsibilities and stop participating in life. It is about you learning the best way to take care of yourself as you move forward. It is about learning to love and cherish yourself, just as your loved one would have wanted you to do.

Being self-compassionate does not mean you never do anything strenuous. The day comes when you need to go back to work, interact with the public, or attend social functions. Self-compassion allows you to be aware of your limitations. To find a way to move forward with your life gently.

As I moved forward on my journey with grief, I realized that I was harboring some resentment toward a couple of people who I felt did not step up to the plate to assist me. I had to sit with this. You might have a situation like this of your own. Death does not always bring out the best in us. You might have friends or relatives who were insensitive during your time of need. And sometimes there is that person who acts up.

Eventually, you realize that these people are just who they are. They have such a fear of death and such discomfort with other people's suffering that they were not fully there for you. Or because they acted out, you wished they had not shown up at all. Begin to work on sending them compassion during your meditations to release your disappointment in their behavior. Just remember, this is not easy for any of us.

A possible next stop on your journey is to help others whose grief is newer and rawer than yours. If you find that someone else's difficult situation brings you challenges, this is an opportunity for growth and learning—to get yourself the support you need. You can start with returning to wishing self-compassion for yourself, and when the time comes that you are no longer triggered by death and grief, turn your compassion toward others.

Working with others who are grieving has taught me an important lesson. Not only is this difficult for all of us, but there are also different degrees of difficulty and suffering. Others have experiences that are entirely different from yours. I will admit, there have been times when I realized that I was being judgmental about how someone was navigating their grief. This part of me just knew how they should act, what they needed to hear, and more. Or I would look at someone and think, "Yes, it is awful that your dog died, but you *should* be able to get up and leave your house and go to work." But one day, it hit me—I was beginning to act in a way that I found objectionable when grieving. It annoyed me when people would come to me and tell me what I should be doing or how I should be acting. How embarrassing, but at the same time, what a fantastic lesson in compassion and understanding the suffering of others.

It does not matter if I think you should be able to get up and go to work the day after your dog has died. It does not matter if I think you should pull it together and go to the grocery store by yourself. What matters is that you are suffering, and it is not my role to judge what is good suffering. To be helpful, I need to understand that you are suffering—and to be compassionate is to see your suffering—wish to alleviate your suffering, and act when I can. Sometimes, the most humane thing I can do is to send you *metta*. With this realization came another component to my death training plan—a reminder that just because I have walked through an experience does not mean I am an expert or stronger or doing a better job. We are not all running the same race, so let's support one another's experiences.

When you can channel the energy of your grief into doing good deeds for others or sending your compassionate thoughts to others, you are creating positive energy and the deceased may benefit from that energy. In this way, you can acknowledge that they are gone, and without attachment, keep them in your heart and do good things in their name. Again, if the conditions are right, the merit you generate on their behalf may find them.

As you grieve, let there be compassion, first for yourself. Later, send compassion to others who were impacted by your loss. And then, when you feel your strength return, remember that everyone will have this experience, and let this realization fill your heart with an abundance of compassion so that it cannot be contained. Your best response is to send that compassion out to all beings.

If, with a mind free from hate,
one arouses love toward just one being,
one thereby becomes good.
Compassionate in mind toward all beings,
The noble one generates abundant merit. (AN 8.1)

WHEN IT COMES TO GRIEF, IT'S COME AS YOU ARE

How did you first learn about death? And by learning about death, I mean when was the first time that death became more than an abstract concept to you? In 2021, as I interviewed 12 wise Buddhist teachers, this was my first question. It seemed like an appropriate segue into a discussion around death Dhamma , and I was sincerely curious. Do some people come with a natural ability to be fully present with death? Two of the 12 did seem to have an innate ability to be with death and dying. With the remaining 10, some had what is considered a traditional introduction:

- Death of a pet during childhood

- Death of an elderly relative during childhood

- Death of a distant friend or family member

- Death that hits closer to home

Some of the group experienced tragic losses at a very young age—a parent or a sibling's death. Due to their shock and inability to handle the situation, the adults around them did not help them process these deaths. One woman, whose father died when she was relatively young, shared that it went like this: her mother said something along the lines of, "Your father died, he is never coming back. Now, eat your dinner." As you can imagine, this woman would not grapple with her father's death for many years. She is not alone; three others shared stories of how death, experienced when we are young or when we do not have the tools or help to cope, can linger for decades or perhaps even an entire lifetime.

We face grief in whatever shape we are in at the time. That is why I so often use the analogy of running a marathon. To complete a marathon takes training. Part of each of our experiences stems from our mental, emotional, and spiritual state. Even those of us who learned about death more gradually could have used some guidance. If adults were able to discuss death with children and were able to teach them that everything—plants, pets, wild animals, and human beings—has a lifecycle, then losing your dog as a child would have been easier. Yes, you would still have been sad. But death would not have seemed like some punishment from on high or some random, unfair event.

One of the 12 wise Buddhist teachers I interviewed identifies as being in addiction recovery. This is who she is, and we are fortunate that she openly shares her experiences and brings them to her practice. She recalls two distinct situations. When her mother died, she was still drinking, and when her brother died, she was sober.

This is how she experienced her mother's death: "I was on the West Coast. She was on the East Coast. I was in college, living with some roommates. When I got home from school. My roommate told me that my brother had called and said that our mother had died. So that was the message: your brother called and said your mom died. And I said, give me a beer because I was not interested in feeling anything."

She went on to say, "Right, so there was no investigation of grief, and I would get angry at people who said I'm sorry about your mom." Her response was to go right to self-medication.

A few years later, her brother died from cancer. "It was night and day because I was experiencing what was my first real intimacy experience; a willingness to be with the feeling of grief, whatever it was to cry in public at the funeral and wake, and so it was really interesting." Her ability to be with grief was a welcome experience. This was the experience that she was not ready to have when her mother died.

She continued: "And I also had another interesting experience, the day of my brother's funeral. He was buried in the morning, and then that evening we were all sitting around. His wife and children and family out back of their house in New Jersey, laughing because we were telling stories. And I remember reflecting, *does this mean I'm not sad,* But then I realized, *no, it's just this moment. In this moment, we're just laughing and then (later) the grief would come, and the joy would go—just the movement of the emotions.* And I realized that, you know, the grief is going to come when it comes."

And it did. Sometimes she would be driving down the road, and all of a sudden, she would think of her brother and burst into tears.

For this wise teacher, acknowledging the grief associated with her parents (who predeceased her brother) occurred while working with her therapist and deepening her Buddhist practice. An important lesson that she conveyed to me during our discussion is that just because there is no grieving does not mean there is no grief. The grief is there. Somehow, you have managed to stuff it away. Eventually, it is going to come crawling out of you. She observed this as she developed a formal meditation practice—the things that she had never tended to surfaced. It was almost as if past experiences would rise to greet her, saying, "*Hello, I'm here*". In this way, she was able to process the grief that she had tried to stuff away.

Your experience with grief is based on your condition. You cannot control when you have to face suffering. You can take control of your preparations. As the Buddha states in more than one passage, *practice ardently*. The time to do so is *now*. The way to do so is to practice consistently. Meditate regularly. Study the teachings. Develop spiritual friendships and join a community. Use the Four Noble Truths and the Noble Eightfold Path to guide how you live your life. That is how you prepare to meet whatever life and death bring your way.

BE YOUR
ALLY IN TIMES OF LOSS

Take a moment to answer this question: "Who is the best person I know who will help me find release from suffering?" Now, expand your answer from the best person to your top three. Did you include yourself on the list? If so, great. If not, I urge you to reconsider! You can be one of your own best resources. Others will be part of your journey, but it is in your best interest to be your own best friend. With that thought in mind, let's consider how you can offer yourself support as you deal with death and grief.

1) Acknowledge your discomfort

Perhaps one of the best ways to help yourself become comfortable with death and grief is to recognize that you are *not* comfortable with death and grief. And do you know what this means? It means that you are normal. Acknowledging your discomfort is the first step toward decreasing the suffering you feel as you grapple with your fear of death, your fear of losing your loved ones, and your own demise.

2) Do what makes sense

In times of your own suffering, remember to be your own best friend. Don't think that you're doing something wrong. Don't beat yourself up over what you're not doing. I am reminded of a discussion I had with the first person I interviewed for the Death Dhamma podcast.

My first podcast guest told me of how, during the AIDS pandemic, he and other volunteers were chastised for assembling safer-sex kits. Their director rebuked them, stating that they should have spent their time differently. The staff therapist stepped in and advised the director that what they were doing was good for their mental health. They were together and having this communal experience of doing something proactive. The repetitive nature of the task helped them process the grief and trauma that they were experiencing.

3) It's OK to just *be*

Another kernel of wisdom that he shared with me was the idea that "we are human *beings*, not human *doings*." This was particularly impactful to me as a person who's always trying to run around being productive. During difficult times, I may seek to relieve my suffering by keeping busy. In the spirit of self-compassion, I accept myself for who I am. Still, it doesn't hurt me to remember that I'm also a *being*, not a *doing*. When you're going through grief, it's okay to *be* and not to worry about how much you *do*. You will do once you give yourself time to be.

4) Pay attention to your internal dialogue

As you feel grief or fear of death, think about how you are expressing yourself, whether through your internal dialogue or in your communications with others. The thoughts you repeat in your head are creating a lasting narrative. And that lasting narrative might tie you further to your own suffering. Last year, I met a man who had lost his partner. She stayed home from work ill and died suddenly and unexpectedly from an aneurysm. A decade later, he referred to this as "the tragedy." Understandably, he loved her so much that her loss was tragic.

One of my wise teachers told me the story of a man who spoke of going through a painful, traumatic divorce. By teaching this man to restate his story, this time without the adjectives, he showed him how to drop the suffering he was carrying around with him. During your difficult times, be aware of the language you use. Be mindful of how you are describing your experience. I will always admire my father for his perspective on his terminal cancer diagnosis. He said, "I never ask 'why me?' Instead, I realize, 'why not me?'"

5) Practice acceptance and gratitude

Another helpful teacher shared that when she needs an immediate way to accept or to intercept painful emotions, she uses this mantra: "Right now, it is like this." This helps her to pause and consider what is happening right now in her body and in her mind, and to accept that whatever she's feeling is okay.

Once you accept your current state, you can access your gratitude practice.

I remember trying to figure out the benefits of having the two people who were closest to me die within a week of each other. The answer came to me as people asked how I was doing. And I would reply, "I am as well-positioned as possible in a difficult situation." This was true. I had a roof over my head, food on the table, and I had other people who cared about me. I had some degree of security. And I didn't have to make big life-changing decisions. The more I looked for things to be grateful for, the more I found. Each day, I challenged myself to come up with three things for which I was grateful. Some days were really difficult. But it was possible to find three things every day, even if on some days I needed to repeat a list from a previous day. This was an exercise in not turning off my sorrow, not turning off my grief, but in bringing myself to accept some gratitude, in turn, helping me to renew and to restore, and providing me some relief from the grief.

6) Go back to the basics

In a discussion on helpful teachings, the first thing one of my colleagues said was, "Go back to the Four Noble Truths." He also reminded me of the five recollections; remember, "I am of the nature to die, there is no way to escape death." These passages, along with the *Maraṇasati Sutta* or mindfulness of death, can be used to remind us of the truth of suffering, the truth of impermanence, and the fact that death is normal and unavoidable.

We will get sick. We will lose things. Our physical and mental state will change. And that understanding isn't intended to bring us more suffering. It is actually intended to help us to come to terms or to peace with what will happen to us. We don't want to be pessimistic, but we do want to be realistic. And in this realism, we will find strength—strength that we find by relying on the teachings, and our Buddhist community, and our practice.

7) Practice consistently

You cannot go back and change the past. You cannot control the future. In this moment, you can be consistent in your practice. When a Sri Lankan monk once said to a group of us, "Be happy and do good and be good, as much as you can. And that is the best way for you to be happy all the time," the monk was not advocating hedonism. He was reminding us to be consistent in our practice. He knew this would bring us peace. Consistent and faithful practice will help you to remain calm. And that peace will help you to be your own your own best resource in your release from suffering.

ON HOMECOMINGS AND RELEASE FROM SUFFERING – NONE OF THIS IS EASY

Today, I find myself thinking of a good friend. Tomorrow, she and her family will bury her father. It will be exactly two weeks since she buried her mother. Toward the end of her mother's service, we stood together, knowing that we would be standing together for a similar reason very soon. Her father was in hospice care and close to death. My friend is strong, resilient, and anchored in her Christian faith. She has difficult days ahead, and she will rise to the occasion.

The fact that her parents had been together for more than 60 years does help us make some sense of the timing. It is not uncommon for older married couples to die within a short period of each other. We understand this, and we tend to console ourselves with the thought that these two people who were like one during life are still together in death. Christian and Buddhist beliefs around what happens after death differ greatly. Some of us will be happy that they have returned home to the Lord, while others will hope they are not returning in rebirth. In both cases, we likely share a sense of relief that the recent deceased does not have to live too long without their partner. A common theme that we all believe is that both of the deceased are now freed from suffering.

At the funeral of my friend's mother, with great conviction and eloquence, the pastor reminded us of the fact that we were gathered together to celebrate a life and a homecoming. A perfect message and statement to his congregation; Christians are not meant to live an earthly life forever. The goal is to go home to the Lord. Standing there as probably the sole Buddhist, I was contemplating rebirth and karma, and eventual freedom from rebirth. These are two very different belief systems. Each can bring the believer some comfort. My friend wants her parents to be reunited with Jesus. I want people to find the ultimate release from suffering.

It is good to have beliefs that give us strength during difficult times and teach us gratitude in times of ease. It is so helpful to know that our deceased loved ones are at peace. To recognize that death is a natural part of the plan—whether you call it God's plan or karma, there will be death. Whether you call it a homecoming or a release from suffering, there is still separation. With the homecoming, there is a leaving. You are left behind.

After my father died, my mother had difficulty living with her grief. Naturally, she turned to her parish priest for guidance. One day, she shared with me that she felt guilty because when the priest told her that she should be glad and joyful that her husband was now with the Lord, she still felt overwhelming sadness. Of course she did. Her best friend and loving partner of almost 55 years was gone. Don't think that I am coming after Christians here, I am not. As a Buddhist, I have been chastised for feeling sadness, because it means that I have not learned to let go of attachment.

None of this easy.

Believing that two people who spent a lifetime together are now together in the afterlife, or working toward a release from suffering, or celebrating a homecoming, all of this is helpful. You will still feel sad. You will recognize that someone you loved is no longer available to you. I hope that what you will not feel is guilt. Specifically, guilt around your grief. Guilt around attachment. You can celebrate a life while experiencing heartache.

Tomorrow, my friend and her siblings and other family members are saying goodbye to their father. It is a time of celebration, of joy, that two people are together in death, and of relief that both mother and father are no longer suffering here on earth. Yet this does not eliminate the difficult emotions. Most of us are not fully ready to lose our parents. It is a strange feeling when your elders are gone. When my last uncle died (my parents predeceased him), one of my cousins commented that now *we* were the elders. I was so confused. How were any of *us* qualified to be the advisers, the ones with life experience? Those who might answer my questions were gone.

We walk through this world with different beliefs, different approaches to processing death, but we share a common humanity. To feel empty or abandoned when both of your parents are gone, these are very human emotions. My hope for my friend, her family, and all of us is that we can celebrate the homecoming, the release from suffering, without hiding our own anguish. To use our beliefs not to mask our sorrow, but to model what it looks like to mourn and all that it entails.

WHO *MOST* DESERVES *YOUR* COMPASSION?

Your best friend is grieving. You don't know how she is going to get through this. She has lost more than one close friend and multiple family members. If ever there was a time to extend compassion, it is now. It's so obvious, isn't it? When someone you love is going through loss and grief, you respond compassionately.

But how do you react when *you* are the one dealing with loss? Don't you deserve compassion? I hope that your friends give you the support you need. Especially your best friend. And by best friend, I mean *you*.

This is a moment of suffering. Suffering is part of life. May I be kind to myself in this moment. May I give myself the compassion I need. — Kristen Neff

You are grieving and you need to treat yourself with compassion. And if you are not sure what that means, or how to begin, please consider these tips:

1. Know your limitations, while gently stretching yourself

Being self-compassionate includes being self-aware and empathetic. For example, early in my grieving process, I would reach a certain point in my day where I was just done; mentally and physically done for the day. The problem was that, initially, this was at about 4 pm. At 4 pm, I felt like I could not do one more thing. I also knew that it was far too early to go to bed. When I felt like I could not do one more thing, I would pick just one more thing to do, and then, after I completed it, I would allow myself to be done for the day. Next, I would meditate. At first, I could only meditate for a few minutes, and it was a major sob fest. But that is OK, I needed those tears.

2. Be mindful of the company you keep

Being self-compassionate includes minimizing the amount of time you spend with people who drain your energy. This is a great rule for us to follow at all times, but now it is even more important. You are running on empty, both physically and emotionally, and you need to take care of yourself first.

Trust your intuition. A friend with whom I had fallen out of touch learned that I was navigating the death of my mother and my husband. The good news for me is that she had forgotten my address. I say that because she began bombarding me with messages about how she needed to come be with me; how I needed someone to come take care of me, and I could not be by myself. In the past, I had watched her method of taking care of others, and while she meant well and had a heart of gold, she was loud and she was overbearing. Her way to take care of someone was to take over every aspect of their life. As an introvert, all I wanted was quiet. I could not imagine having someone in the house with me, telling me what was best for me.

3. Silence your inner critic

You would think that during a time such as this, your inner critic would just be quiet. But that's not what inner critics do, is it? Your inner critic might be telling you things like:

"You should stop crying so much."

"Why aren't you crying more? What's wrong with you?"

"You should be able to concentrate on your work."

"You should be more productive."

"You should, you should, you should . . ."

There is no such thing as *should*, there is only what *is*. Pay close attention to what you are feeling. Accept yourself and your feelings as they are.

4. Don't use self-compassion as an excuse for bad behavior

Being self-compassionate is not a free pass to being self-destructive. It does not mean that it is OK to eat a pint of ice cream every day or to drink a pint of vodka every day. Keep an eye out for self-destructive behaviors.

You still have responsibilities and you will handle those responsibilities. This is the time to sort through the difference between what are nice things to do and what are required things for you to do. Paying your rent or your mortgage, let's call that required. Going to an event because someone said it would be good for you, let's call that optional.

Being self-compassionate does not mean you never do anything difficult. The day comes when you need to go back to work, or interact with the public, or attend social functions. This takes us back to point No. 1: Know your limitations, while gently stretching yourself.

5. Find a way to stay engaged with day-to-day living

You are going to have days when all you want to do is stay under the covers. This is normal. Allow yourself a day to mope. However, do not allow yourself to spend seven days a week under the covers. Most days, you want to get out of bed at a normal time and get dressed. Groom yourself, whether you are leaving the house or not. Eat healthy meals. Resume your exercise routine. Keep in touch with the right people, the people who do not drain your energy (see No. 2: Be mindful of the company you keep). If you have severe difficulties getting up and getting dressed and handling day-to-day living, then get help. Seek out grief support groups and counseling. Ask trusted friends for help. Nobody said you have to go through this alone.

6. Welcome grief into your life

Grief is now a part of your life. In the same way that you might live with allergies or migraines or other challenges, now you live with grief. Just like you have learned to work with your allergies or your migraines or your sensitive stomach, you will learn how to accommodate your grief. I found that I was able to return to teaching within a week. On my way to teaching, I would cry in the car on the way to class. When I was in front of my students, I was able to concentrate on them and, for that short period of time, I was able to forget about my sadness. Once I left the classroom and got back in my car, I would cry all the way home. I learned to keep a good supply of tissues and eye makeup with me at all times. And I learned not to judge myself for needing to cry. Living my life was not about denying the grief; it was about supporting myself in a way that I could get back to the business of living, and, for me, the business of living included making room for grieving.

7. Don't impose an end date on your grief

Even while I was teaching others how to plan and schedule and meet deadlines, I began to realize that there is no specific timeline for grief. There is no magic date on which your sadness expires. As you move forward, your days will be different. Your grief will change from a sharp stabbing pain to a dull ache. Do not let anyone tell you when you should "get over it." Everyone's path is different.

8. Be your own best friend

You are the one who knows yourself the best. Be kind. Do not use your self-talk to say things that you would not say to others. Your best friend is grieving, and she or he above all others deserves your compassion.

Chapter 6

Everyday Dharma: Lessons from Life

———•———

Buddhist wisdom doesn't just visit you on the meditation cushion. It's alive in every moment you breathe, every step you take. Here, you are invited to discover how the fabric of daily life, the warmth of your connections, and the echoes of your memories can become your most profound teachers.

- In the ordinary rhythms of morning light, a shared meal, or the hum of a busy street, you glimpse impermanence, compassion, and mindfulness unfolding naturally. Each small moment reminds you that nothing stays the same—and in that flow lies deep insight.

- Your relationships—with friends, family, even the animals you cherish—offer endless opportunities to loosen the grip of attachment and open your heart in loving-kindness. As you connect, you learn how to give and receive care without clinging.

- And then there are memories: gentle echoes of joy and sorrow that can soothe your wounds and rekindle your wonder at life's beauty. By honoring what has been, you will find healing and a renewed sense of gratitude for the present.

May you be inspired to find Buddhist teachings as a guiding presence in every day, and in each aspect of your life.

KEEP YOUR EYES ON YOUR OWN PAPER

"Girls! Keep your eyes on your own papers!" Sister Mary Angela bellowed while she loomed over us.

Sister Mary Angela, who was in her mid-80s, pulled herself up to her full height of four feet and seven inches, and about 85 pounds. Don't misunderstand, she was a force to be reckoned with. As tiny as she was, I was terrified of her. One of our recent encounters ended with her punching me in the stomach one day because I was not walking to class fast enough.

If she said that she would flunk me if she caught me looking at someone else's paper, then I did not doubt that she would flunk me. My parents would kill me, and I would become a high school dropout and never make it to college. And if I never made it to college, well, all I knew was that it would be bad. OK, I did not think through the part where if my parents killed me, then the rest would not matter. These are the dramatic thoughts I had as a teenage girl. A teenage girl who had yet to encounter Buddhism.

I was so nervous that I didn't even look at the back of the head of the girl in front of me. It didn't even occur to me that this threat was not applicable to me—I actually enjoyed history class and was well-prepared for the exam.

And you know, I didn't turn and look when someone sitting next to me kept whispering, "What's the answer to question five?" I wasn't going to get caught in a trap, oh no.

So, what does this tiny, elderly Catholic nun have to do with Buddhism and grief and Death Dhamma?

In your practice and on your grief journey, keep your eyes on your own paper. As you work on making friends with death and impermanence, keep your eyes on your own paper. Your journey is your journey; your experience is your experience.

Now, let me give you a quote from another Catholic woman, my mother, Joannie Meloni:

"Comparisons are odious."

You might watch someone else who is going through grief and become envious of how she seems to be completely recovered. Perhaps she appears to have absolutely no suffering. You might perceive another person as being too emotional or taking too long to return to normal. You think that she should be able to go to the grocery store without crying.

Stop it. When you compare yourself to others, you will probably either:

1. Feel Superior

2. Feel Inferior

3. Feel equal

If you develop feelings of superiority, you are feeding your ego and opening the door to pride and conceit. If you feel inferior, then you are succumbing to low self-esteem, another form of ego. Even feelings of equality are still feeding into a sense of self. Each of these potential outcomes solidifies a sense of self. Your grief and how you respond to it is not you.

Grief arises in you; you are not grief. Comparing yourself to others, no matter the outcome, is a form of conceit:

"If one regards himself superior or equal or inferior by reason of the body that is impermanent, painful, and subject to change, what else is it than not seeing reality? Or if one regards himself as superior or equal or inferior by reason of feelings, perceptions, volitions, or consciousness, what else is it than not seeing reality? If one does not regard himself superior or equal or inferior by reason of the body, the feelings, perceptions, volitions, or consciousness, what else is it than seeing reality?"(SN 22.49)

The passage above refers to using the body as a basis for feelings of superiority, or inferiority, or equality. You can therefore extrapolate that whatever you use as a basis of comparison is also impermanent. And as such, you are not seeing reality.

None of this is meant to imply that you cannot learn from the experiences of others. If someone you know has a habit, or a credible teaching/teacher, this is worthy of investigation, and if your research brings you new ways to support yourself, try those approaches. But don't compare your results to the results of others. You are not running a time trial; you are not racing to a finish line. Doing a better job than someone else is not a true measurement of your spiritual progress. And what does it mean to do a better job than someone else? Do you meditate longer? Do you meditate more frequently? Do you cry less often?

It is like reading the warning and recommendations on a bottle of medicine: results may vary. Results *will* vary. What matters is *your* progress. Use your energy to discern what works for you, remembering that each day will be different. *Your* experience with *your* grief will vary. You are engaged in a long-term effort. Keep your eyes, your focus, your effort on your own development.

WHAT YOU HAVE IS NOW

In difficult times, it is so easy to time travel. I don't mean with an actual time machine; I mean with your mind. When you are sitting with loss and grief, you might wish that you were anywhere else. Because right here, right now, it's painful. And there were times in the past that were not painful. And you believe that, eventually, at some future point, it will not be painful. And so you time travel: you spend your time revisiting happy memories, or you daydream about a future filled with love and laughter. Perhaps your future will hold love and laughter, but how do you get there? If you don't dwell in the now, then you cannot properly acknowledge your difficult feelings. While the future is not guaranteed, if it does arrive, it will not be joyful if you have not dealt with your pain. If you spend today in the right way, you can have an auspicious day, as the Buddha describes in the *Bhaddekaratta Sutta* (MN 131):

You shouldn't chase after the past.
or place expectations on the future.
What is past?
is left behind.

The future is as yet unreached.
Whatever quality is present.
you clearly see right there,
right there.

Not taken in,
unshaken,
that's how you develop the heart.

Ardently doing
what should be done today,
for—who knows?—tomorrow
death.

There is no bargaining
with Mortality & his mighty horde.

Whoever lives thus ardently,
relentlessly
both day & night,
has truly had an auspicious day:
so says the Peaceful Sage.

By reflecting on this passage, you are reminded that dwelling on the past or fixating on the future only leads to suffering. Instead, you can focus on the present moment and embrace the practice of letting go. Feel the rising and falling of the difficult emotions. There is nothing in the past for you. You do not need to engage in chasing after the past, as the Buddha describes below:

And how, monks, does one chase after the past? One gets carried away with the delight of 'In the past I had such a form (body)'... 'In the past I had such a feeling'... 'In the past I had such a perception'... 'In the past

I had such a thought-fabrication' . . . *'In the past I had such a consciousness.' This is called chasing after the past.*

Likewise, you do not need to place expectations on the future like this:

And how does one place expectations on the future? One gets carried away with the delight of 'In the future I might have such a form (body)'. . . 'In the future I might have such a feeling' . . . 'In the future I might have such a perception' . . . 'In the future I might have such a thought-fabrication' . . . 'In the future I might have such a consciousness.' This is called placing expectations on the future.

Overly anticipating the future and becoming attached to specific outcomes contribute to your suffering. If you want to look forward to a future without suffering, then look to today. And this too must be handled in the right way. The sutta also discusses what "not taken in" means. To have that auspicious day is not just about not chasing the past or the future; it is also about a proper mindset in the present. The Buddha describes one who is not taken in:

And how is one not taken in with regard to present qualities? There is the case where a disciple of the noble ones who has seen the noble ones, is versed in the teachings of the noble ones, is well-trained in the teachings of the noble ones, does not see form as self, or self as possessing form, or form as in self, or self as in form.

It is not just to be in the present moment with your feelings. I am drawing on this idea to make a certain point. In times of difficulty and loss, do not look backward or forward. It is tempting to want to take yourself far away from this painful moment in time. You need to be in the present moment in the right way. Drawing on the Dhamma and working with an understanding that these feelings are not you. You will be confronted by your past, and you are facing your future. But do not squander what you have—and what you have is now. Right now, right in front of you, this is your practice. And, in the overall spirit of Death Dhamma, "Who knows, maybe tomorrow death will come."

REMEMBERING THE WHOLE PERSON: HONOR AND CELEBRATE THE LIFE OF A LOVED ONE

At funerals and memorial services, it is traditional for friends and family members to eulogize their dead loved one. These stories are meant to ease the suffering of those who have been left behind. There are family photos and retellings of stories that are intended to paint a picture of the deceased. A positive, happy picture of the deceased. And on that day, when everyone has gathered together to share their loss, it makes sense that the stories will inspire tears and laughter. Or the occasional "who was that person?" and "why is he speaking about my mother?" It is very rare for someone to stand up and tell the room that the dearly departed was rude or selfish or a liar. It's just not considered to be acceptable behavior. When it does happen, it is likely to make the local news or make the rounds on social media. After the service, as you continue your grief journey, it is important to remember the whole person. While it can be tempting to sugarcoat the memories of our lost loved ones, being honest about their strengths and weaknesses, and remembering the good and the bad, can be an important part of grieving and allow us to move forward.

Be honest about who your loved one was

Remembering the dead is not mere nostalgia, but a profound spiritual practice. To remember them is to keep their spirit alive and find new meaning in their lives. (Ajahn Chah)

It is important to be honest about the way your loved one was before they passed away. While it may be difficult to speak about the less-than-ideal qualities of the deceased, it is important to remember that this is a part of who they were, and telling the truth about their life can be a powerful way to honor them. Sharing stories of both the good and difficult times can be a way of acknowledging all that they were.

My mother was sometimes difficult. Well, if you did not do things her way, she was difficult. She was a bit dramatic, a bit of a hypochondriac, and could be selfish. She liked to be the center of attention. When she died, five days before my husband died, a friend who knew my mother said, "That makes perfect sense; she was not going to let him take all of the attention." And then we looked at each other and laughed. Not in a mean-spirited way. But rather in a "what are you going to do about it?" type of way.

There is more to us than just our bad qualities. Remembering that your loved one was charismatic, funny, or had a great sense of humor can help lighten the mood and allow you to remember the most positive aspects of their life. Additionally, take time to recognize the values they stood for and the traits they exhibited that you hope to emulate in your own life.

I loved my mother, difficulties and all. She was smart, independent, and well-read. She had a beautiful singing voice. She was amazing at the home arts. Long before we had TV shows and books about home chefs and talented homemakers, my mother was making us cloth napkins and making our clothing and cutting our hair and treating us to homemade meals that rivaled any Michelin-starred restaurant. She was an amazing hostess and loved entertaining. She had impeccable manners. In her later years, she became a master gardener. I can look at all her talents and see the positive influences she had on me.

When you say something negative about the dead

Not everyone is open to your truthful acceptance of the negative traits of your dead loved one. It is likely that some of you have already thought "how could she say those things about her dead mother?"

I learned this lesson the hard way. One day, I was doing some gardening in my front yard (see, thanks, Mom). A neighbor walked by and said, "I bet you miss having Ed out here to help you." Without thinking, I replied, "You mean to sit on the wall and drink coffee and watch me work?"

That's how it was. Ed did not like doing yard work. But he did like spending time with me. His way of participating was to come out and keep me company. That was our routine. And it was mostly great. Ok, once in a while, when he started giving me directions about where to plant which flower, I might have become a tad grumpy. Also, his thoughts about where to plant the flower were usually right on target. He was always better at aesthetics.

But my neighbor did not know the whole part of why I responded that way I did. And in her mind, I was being mean-spirited toward my dead husband. It was unfortunate that my reply came across as negative, but to me, I was remembering the entirety of our time together in the front yard.

It is important to be mindful of the reactions that your words may have on others. Some people may take offense to any negative words spoken about the deceased, while others may view it as an opportunity to remember the person in their entirety. Now, I am very careful about how I share memories and with whom I share them.

The importance of not glorifying the dead

Speaking negatively about the deceased does not mean that you did not love or appreciate them. Speaking honestly about the person is sometimes the best way to honor them, and it is important to remember that you can still love someone even if you recognize their flaws. Our ability to love one another in all of our imperfections speaks highly of all of us.

Your loved one was a real person with both successes and failures. Glorifying the dead can sometimes do a disservice to those who are remembering them. Allowing yourself to recognize and remember both the good and the bad can be an important part of the grieving process. While it can be difficult to recognize the mistakes made by your loved one, it is important to remember that they were still a person, and they were still important.

If you only remember your deceased as perfect. You are less likely to feel motivated to act on their behalf. I am specifically referring to earning and transferring merit. Remember that your actions in this world can help your loved one with a more positive rebirth. Acknowledging that perhaps your dead family member has not achieved nirvana is good motivation to do good and to dedicate the fruits of your merit.

Remember the whole person

Remembering the dead is a great act of loving-kindness. (Ajahn Sulak Sivaraksa)

When remembering a loved one after their death, it is important to remember the whole person. While it can be tempting to sugarcoat their memories, taking the time to speak honestly about both the good and the bad can be an important part of the healing process.

Be mindful of the words you choose, as it may affect the way others remember the deceased. Taking the time to remember a loved one in their entirety is an important part of honoring and celebrating their life.

THE PERFECT WAY TO COMMEMORATE A DEATH DAY

Her phone pinged, and Mary Carol looked down to read the following text message:

Hey Mary Carol, I am thinking of you today. I know it is a very difficult and sad day for you. Today is his death day. Your husband and my best friend left us two years ago.

As she read the text, Mary Carol was not sure how she felt. She was not sure how she was supposed to feel. That's not true; she felt guilty. It's not that she hadn't remembered that it was the anniversary of his death; it was that when she received the text, she was enjoying a happy, peaceful day with one of her best friends. Her friend noticed the change in Mary Carol's demeanor and asked her what was wrong. Mary Carol shrugged and showed her friend the text.

Now it was her friend's turn to feel guilty as she looked at Mary Carol and said, "I'm sorry, I forgot. I knew it was around this time of year, but I did not remember his actual death date." Together they fell silent, and then they went right back to what they had been doing—catching up with one another and going back to their activity.

After a while, Mary Carol told her friend that she wanted to make a phone call. She realized that she needed to touch base with her deceased husband's best friend. She believed that the text was as much for him as it was for her. On that day, she had plans and felt strong and protected. But what about her husband's best friend? That text was very possibly his way of reaching out and saying, "Hey, I am sad, today I miss my best friend." And sure enough, that short phone call was beneficial to both of them, a strengthening of their bond, and a reminder of someone they loved.

Later, Mary Carol would have plenty of time to reflect on her feelings and how she wanted to commemorate the death dates of her husband and her other loved ones. She learned that she did not necessarily feel the need to set aside time on the anniversaries of her parents' deaths, or of her husband's death, or of anyone's death. On those days, she would remember. She would probably spend a few minutes in contemplation or dedicate some extra time in her meditation practice. Her preference was to live those days as if they were any other day, carrying about the business of life.

Some of her friends came from traditions that celebrate the anniversary of a death. Putting up pictures and creating an altar to show respect for the dead. During a time around the death day, they might have a special meal or cook some of the deceased's favorite foods. Another friend used social media to post images from the past and to remind others that this was the time when her partner died. And yet another friend would refuse to interact with others because this was her time to be sad.

Do you see a pattern? The pattern is that we all find our own ways to handle death days. There is no one perfect way to recognize a death day. And with no one clear answer, you have permission to create your ritual, or lack thereof. You also have permission to honor different death days differently, perhaps baking something special on your mother's death day and watching your father's favorite movie on his death day. And maybe next year, you do the same thing, or nothing. It does not matter how many years it has been. Let your feelings guide you. Give yourself some loving-kindness and compassion.

How can we best support one another? With loving-kindness and compassion, and by selecting actions to care for one another. If you know that your friend has a death day approaching, but you are not sure how they are spending this day, reach out from a place of respect. If you feel that you have the type of relationship where you can ask, "Hey, what are you doing on your father's death day?" Then do so. If you feel uncertain, then send a card, or drop off a meal, or some treats, or meet for a walk or coffee. Maybe you send a text, like this one,

Hey Mary Carol, I am thinking of you today. I know it is a very difficult and sad day for you. Today is his death day. Your husband and my best friend left us two years ago.

Most importantly, seek to suspend all judgment. Your way of handling a death day is your way. When it is your turn, you will honor your loved ones the best way that you can, and I hope that your living friends and family respect your way, with love and compassion.

WHOSE KARMA IS THIS?

Is the death of my loved ones my karma or theirs? Our lives were intertwined, and so is our karma. When my mother and my husband died just five days apart, some told me that I must have had some really bad karma to have lost the two people I was closest to during the same time frame. There was nothing particularly helpful about these comments. Eventually, I realized that these comments were probably not meant to be judgments about me; they were meant to make others feel better about their own lives. If they could convince themselves that I have some really bad karma, they could better come to terms with what had happened. They could seek to assure themselves that something like this would not happen to them.

Is it possible that my father and my husband, Ed, had karmic similarities? Within two years of one another, they both died from the same form of lung cancer. At some point in their lives, both of them had smoked. Lung cancer was in my father's genetic makeup. His brother, Bill, died four years later, also of lung cancer. My grandfather battled lung cancer. Some might call this an interesting twist of fate. I have learned to call it karma. Is it my karma to have loved individuals who would have had lung cancer? Absolutely. But my experience is not unique. In the United States, an estimated 131,880 people will die from lung cancer in 2021.* Lung cancer and losing family and friends to lung cancer is part of our karma.

Karma—kamma in Pāli—is a complicated topic. In its simplest form, it means action. In today's world, especially in the West, many see it as payback or retribution. We see too many bumper stickers and t-shirts that say, "Karma's a bitch." In our culture, there are not enough acknowledgments of good karma and not enough recognition that "Instant Karma" might be a catchy song by John Lennon, but it's not an accurate representation of what we should expect in the real world.

If you find yourself wanting someone to be punished for their bad acts, be careful. You are falling into the trap of wishing them ill will. And your intention creates your karma. You will see people perform the same actions and appear to receive different results. This could be true. It can also mean that the karma from a particular action will ripen at another time.

AN 3.99, the *Lonaphala Sutta* teaches us that some people will perform the same action with different karmic results:

"There is the case where a trifling evil deed done by a certain individual takes him to hell. There is the case where the very same sort of trifling deed done by another individual is experienced in the here and now, and for the most part barely appears for a moment."

And the reason for these different results has to do with how you have developed yourself:

"Now, a trifling evil deed done by what sort of individual takes him to hell? There is the case where a certain individual is undeveloped in

[contemplating] the body, undeveloped in virtue, undeveloped in mind, undeveloped in discernment: restricted, small-hearted, dwelling with suffering. A trifling evil deed done by this sort of individual takes him to hell.

"Now, a trifling evil deed done by what sort of individual is experienced in the here & now, and for the most part barely appears for a moment? There is the case where a certain individual is developed in [contemplating] the body, developed in virtue, developed in mind, developed in discernment: unrestricted, large-hearted, dwelling with the immeasurable.[1] A trifling evil deed done by this sort of individual is experienced in the here & now, and for the most part barely appears for a moment."

Was I a bad person in a past life? This is an unanswerable question. And anyway, there is nothing I can do about my past lives. All I can do is work to be the best person that I can be *now*. The karma that I experience is a blend of my past and current actions.

I cannot go back in time and change anything about my current or past lives. Time travel storylines, while fun, are inherently flawed. You are only supposed to change one thing, but if you change other things, the universe is cursed forever. You are never supposed to meet yourself in another dimension, or the universe is cursed forever. Forget about all that. It is much easier to just work on your life as you live it *right now*.

You do not know what will come. You *do* know that whatever happens is part of *your* karma. There is no need to rush through any part of your life;

it is all as it is meant to be. Just keep practicing; do not spend time trying to predict how your karma will ripen.

The *Acintita Sutta* (AN 4.77) says:

"There are these four unconjecturables that are not to be conjectured about, that would bring madness and vexation to anyone who conjectured about them. Which four?"

The sutta goes on to state that the precise working out of the results of karma is one of the four things not to be conjectured about.

It never occurred to me to ask *why* my family members died when they did. To practice Buddhism is to accept impermanence and to know that your karma cannot be fully mapped out, nor predicted. To fully embrace impermanence is to understand that everything that arises will cease. *Everything* also means *everyone*. We are *all* going to die, and we are *all* going to lose people we love. This is part of our karma.

* Key Statistics for Lung Cancer (American Cancer Society)

OF RAINBOWS AND SEA TURTLES: LETTING MEMORIES GUIDE AND HEAL US

It was my last morning on the island. A long walk was in order. Not just to burn off my lack of discipline at the breakfast buffet, but to enjoy a good stretch before I sat for hours on the flight home. I also wanted to spend as much time as possible enjoying the natural beauty that surrounded me.

As I stood watching the waves break over an outcropping of lava rock, I noticed that one of the rocks was not like the others. It was smoother and had a different shape and texture. Then I realized: "That's no rock, that's a sea turtle!" This brought a smile to my face, as I had yet to spot a sea turtle during this visit, and because the sea turtle brought back happy memories.

I recall powering up the desktop computer that my husband Ed and I shared. I noticed that the avatar I normally clicked on to take me to my files and folders had been replaced by the picture of a turtle. At first, I was taken aback. "A turtle? He thinks I look like a turtle?" Then I understood. The first time we visited Hawaii together, we had checked into our hotel, left our baggage in our room, and went to the water as fast as possible. We walked around a small lagoon and spotted it, our first sea turtle! That explained the turtle avatar. Later, I presented my turtle avatar theory to him, and he smiled and nodded. He was a wise man, so if I was wrong and for some other reason, I reminded him of a turtle, he was not going to disturb our peace.

The last time that we visited Hawaii together, we arrived with heavy hearts. Just two months prior, my father had died. We had spent much of that time traveling back and forth between our home in Southern California and my parents' home in Washington State. My mother was not yet ready to be alone. We would alternate—one of us staying in California while the other would stay in Washington. Sometimes, we would pass each other on the road in Washington, one on the way to the airport, the other on the way from the airport. We were fortunate to be able to provide Mom with this type of support. Still, we were exhausted.

There we were, sad and overwhelmed, staring at the water and the palm trees. And then it appeared a large, well-formed rainbow. We both came from traditions that taught that the rainbow was God's promise. We also both left those traditions for Buddhism. Still, this rainbow gave us both a sense of hope and peace.

Sea turtles and rainbows are not particularly rare in Hawaii. Depending on when and where you visit, you will probably see a turtle and a rainbow more than once. I don't think that my deceased husband sent the turtle I recently saw. I don't think that my late father created the rainbow. But I have come to understand that no matter how long someone has been gone, there will be times when you encounter a person, place, or thing that will bring you back to a time when your loved one was still alive. Treat these moments as gifts, even if they bring tears to your eyes. Accept a flashback as a helpful tool. Watch the memories as they arise within you, note the feelings that surface, and as the memory fades away, let it go. Look at that sea turtle, smile at that sea turtle, maybe even take a picture—because you can't have too many pictures of sea turtles. Then, continue your walk. Return to the present and live life as it is now.

There is the potential for stressful, traumatic memories to surface. Maybe you see a car that reminds you of unhappy family road trips. The kind where one or both of your parents said to you and your brothers or sisters, "Don't make me pull this car over!" Unfortunately, you and your siblings continued to act up and once the car was pulled over, you received a spanking. That's not the best memory. In a way, these difficult memories can still be a gift. They show you where you have some work to do with forgiveness or processing trauma and difficult emotions. Just like with the happy memories, watch the memory arise within you, note how you feel, and let the memory go. If you find that you are unable to let go, or that dread and anxiety remain behind, be sure to seek professional help.

Accept the fact that memories will come. You do not always know when, where, or why. You do know that these memories are another opportunity to practice.

SOMETHING IS MISSING, BECAUSE SOMEONE IS MISSING

Wait a minute, something feels off. You know that something is missing, but it's not immediately obvious. And then it hits you: this is exactly where you would have asked your father for advice. But you can't. At least not in any traditional way. And the reason that you cannot just call your father on the phone is that he is dead.

This is not new information to you. Logically, you know he is dead. You have accepted this.

You have learned to live without the daily messages of encouragement and the occasional silly joke that makes you groan. You understand that you will not see your father on his birthday or your birthday. You have gotten to a point where, when you wake up in the morning, you don't have to remind yourself that he is dead. Once in a while, you feel his loss differently. It is not the same as the sharp pangs of sadness you felt at an earlier point in your grief journey. Now, you are recognizing a different type of loss. In this case, you have lost a trusted mentor.

As you traverse your grief journey, you begin to notice different types of losses that come with the death of your loved one. The first and most obvious is that this person is gone, no longer alive; he/she/they will not walk into the room or see you at dinner. You will experience other forms of loss. Here, in no particular order, is what you might experience.

The memories, routines, and shared moments that once defined your life together are gone. The meals you enjoyed, the conversations you had, the inside jokes that only the two of you understood, they are now just bittersweet memories. Until you re-establish your routine and create shared moments with others, you will feel a sense of incompleteness. When you spend time with others, you may still feel the absence of your loved one. Don't rush to fill that space; be cautious and treat yourself tenderly. Empty space (not the same thing as emptiness) is better than toxic space. Be discerning in the company you keep.

You had a sense of self that included another person. Their death means the loss of a part of your identity. You were a partner, or a friend, or a child. Now, who are you? You have lost a part of yourself. The roles and responsibilities that defined you in the context of that relationship are suddenly upended. You may find yourself questioning who you are without them, feeling adrift in a sea of uncertainty. This loss of identity can be disorienting, requiring you to redefine yourself in a world that no longer includes your loved one. Take your time and seek to embrace not knowing. Do not be too quick to create a new you. Work on accepting the fact that there are aspects of who you are that will be re-established. There are roles that you might need to let go. You did have a father, and you were his child. Your father's death does not negate that fact, but it does mean that you no longer have an active parent-child relationship.

Along with a change in your identity can come a change in the stability of your life. This might be a financial issue or an emotional issue. Especially if the person who died is the person you most relied on to help you through difficult times. Or who supported you financially. I recall that when my mother died, I would have relied on my husband for emotional support, and when my husband died, I would have relied on my mother for emotional support. They died within five days of one another, leaving me to depend on others. The good news is that friends stepped in to help me. Be open to the loving and well-intentioned support of others. The type of assistance that does not come with expectations of reciprocity.

When your life changes, your life changes. That may seem like an obvious statement. You have so much change when someone close to you dies. Your social network, your connections, and your support networks are going to be different. This might be immediately true, as someone you expect to be there is unable to show up because death is something he, she, or they are not prepared to handle. Next will be a person(s) who supports you for a while and then steps back, and, eventually, others may leave as they grapple with who you are becoming. Some people will have strong ideas about what your new life is meant to be, and you might make different choices. Make the choices that support you and know that you might lose people. There might be a time when some of your old friends are no longer with you. As you create your new life, you will form new friendships.

This grief journey is not easy. You find yourself grappling with feelings of emptiness, insecurity, and a sense of being adrift. As you recognize new forms of loss and change, you will need to find new ways to live, new ways to feel safe and supported. You do not have to walk alone. Rely on your practice, find others on the path, a strong teacher, and professional help if you feel overwhelmed.

Conclusion

This is not really the end. There is no end. Even when you die, and others mourn you, the journey continues. If you have lived your last life, then you will not return. But others keep you alive in their own way, just as you honor your dead loved ones, and make them part of your life.

To quote George Eliot, 'Our dead are never dead to us, until we have forgotten them.'

We are all in various stages of our grief journeys. If you have never lost a loved one, never been disappointed in life, or let go of a dream or a relationship, then you are just setting out. The rest of us are out here, moving along at our own pace. I hope that reading all or some of these articles has shown you that there are many ways to grieve, there is no perfect schedule, and grief will always be part of your life. There is no one way to honor your dead family and friends. This is not meant to be discouraging. Rather, it is meant to encourage you to acknowledge grief, make space for it in your life, just as you make space for fun and joy and celebrations.

If there is any 'right way,' it would be the Four Noble Truths and the Noble Eightfold Path. This excerpt from the *Sammādiṭṭhi* Sutta: The Discourse on Right View helps to make the connection.

"When, friends, a noble disciple understands aging and death, the origin of aging and death, the cessation of aging and death, and the way leading to the cessation of aging and death, in that way he is one of right view... and has arrived at this true Dhamma.

"And what is aging and death, what is the origin of aging and death, what is the cessation of aging and death, what is the way leading to the cessation of aging and death? The aging of beings in the various orders of beings, their old age, brokenness of teeth, grayness of hair, wrinkling of skin, decline of life, weakness of faculties — this is called aging. The passing of beings out of the various orders of beings, their passing away, dissolution, disappearance, dying, completion of time, dissolution of the aggregates, laying down of the body — this is called death. So this aging and this death are what is called aging and death. With the arising of birth there is the arising of aging and death. With the cessation of birth there is the cessation of aging and death. The way leading to the cessation of aging and death is just this Noble Eightfold Path; that is, right view... right concentration.

"When a noble disciple has thus understood aging and death, the origin of aging and death, the cessation of aging and death, and the way leading to the cessation of aging and death... he here and now makes an end of suffering. In that way too a noble disciple is one of right view... and has arrived at this true Dhamma". – MN 9

Thank you for trusting me with your time, your heart, and your practice. A special thank you to Buddhistdoor Global for allowing me to share Death Dhamma with your audience. May we all be well and happy, at peace, and free from suffering. See you along the path!

Margaret Meloni
www.margaretmeloni.com

www.ingramcontent.com/pod-product-compliance
Lightning Source LLC
Chambersburg PA
CBHW052142070526
44585CB00017B/1936